THE
TECHNIQUES
OF
WORKING WITH
THE WORKING PRESS

by

HAL GOLDEN
Director of Public Relations
Greater New York Fund

and

KITTY HANSON
Reporter-Feature Writer
New York Daily News

Oceana Publications, Inc.

Dobbs Ferry, N. Y.

62,499

To
Christina

BOOKS BY

Hal Golden & Kitty Hanson

How To Plan, Produce and Publicize
SPECIAL EVENTS

The Techniques of
WORKING WITH THE WORKING PRESS

PREFACE

I HAVE READ "The Techniques of Working With the Working Press" with much interest. It is by far the best book in its field with which I am familiar. It is packed with solid information clearly expressed. I am sure it will be an invaluable tool to anyone—amateur or professional—who wants to get information about a particular subject into his newspaper.

FRANK S. ADAMS
City Editor
The New York Times

ACKNOWLEDGMENTS

WE WISH TO extend our sincere thanks to the many men and women of the newspaper business and many organizations who gave us their time and advice so generously during the researching of this book. Their response, by letter, by telephone and in person, was gratifying evidence of their belief in the need for this book.

We are indebted to *Editor and Publisher* magazine, a fount of informational material; to *Business Management* magazine, *PR Reporter*, *Public Relations Journal*, *PR Quarterly*, *Printer's Ink* magazine, and *Channels*.

We are also indebted to two very important Richards: to Richard W. Clarke, Editor of *The New York Daily News*, for his interest and assistance; to Richard E. Booth, Executive Director of the Greater New York Fund, for his support and confidence.

CONTENTS

1

WHY THIS BOOK?

DESPITE THE phenomenal growth of television and the TV audience, the printed word in the newspaper is still the most powerful voice in the world of communications.

Although radio and television are important media to the man with a product or an idea to sell, and although an advertisement may be able to make the sales pitch with more ballyhoo and less modesty, nothing has yet come along to challenge the weight and influence of a few printed lines in the news columns of the local newspaper.

"I saw it in the paper" has settled more arguments than the National Labor Relations Board and influenced more people than Dale Carnegie. It is small wonder that the daily newspaper remains the Number One prestige medium for the placement of publicity.

Newspapers have for years enjoyed this virtually unchallenged position within their communities and, by building large circulations and strong reader loyalties, have become a powerful voice in the affairs of the entire country. More than 107 million Americans over the age of twelve read some newspaper every day. That's a readership that spends a billion-and-a-half dollars a year on newspapers alone and adds up to nearly 85 per cent of the population.

Unlike other important and influential industries, however, only the newspaper industry is a target for the daily unremitting onslaught of intruders—men and women who represent an incredible diversity of special interests outside the newspaper business.

Into newspaper offices throughout the country every day pour releases, letters, telegrams, telephone calls, and visitors—all with one thing in common: A request for free editorial space or some other kind of special consideration. Some of the requests are made directly to the editor or reporter; others come in through the back door by way of an advertising salesman, circulation manager, secretary or friend-of-a friend. They come from commerce and industry, civic groups, non-profit organizations, and individuals.

Often the representative of a special interest is a professional publicity man who holds a salaried position and has a specific responsibility to get his client or his organization into print. More often, however, he is an unpaid non-professional—the butcher, the baker, the candlestick maker—someone with little or no training in publicity who has been assigned a publicity job for a baker's dozen of unrelated reasons.

To most newspapermen, these special interest spokesmen are a major source of irritation—not because they've sworn a solemn oath to hate all publicity people (some of their best friends are press agents), but because so few publicity men really understand what makes a newspaper tick. This is true of the professionals who earn a living in the business as of the housewife who finds she is this year's publicity chairman for the Garden Club.

In their dealings with the newspaper and with newspapermen, too many of these amateur and professional publicists ignore or overlook the most basic requirements of the newspaper business.

There are many good reasons (although no excuses) for this failure on the part of publicity people. Many publicity men receive their basic training in areas foreign to journalism—in advertising, sales, personnel, and the like. In fact, top public relations jobs in some of the country's leading corporations are often filled with executives trained, not in public relations, but in accounting, law, or general business administration. Management, which has accepted the role of public relations in business, still does not fully understand this profession which deals somewhat in the area of intangibles. So, in recruiting men for the top public relations job, it seeks out specialists in the tangibles in the hope of giving this area a greater feeling of stability. This may appease management's lack of understanding and confidence in public relations, but it does little to improve the public relations job the company is trying to do.

Another reason why some publicity men fail to satisfy the needs of the responsible press is that many of them have graduated out of the highly specialized school of press agentry. Here is one phase of the publicity business where the only working ground rule is "the more flamboyant the better." Unfortunately, although the practioners may have been graduated from press agentry to press relations, their techniques have not.

There are many talented and creative people in this area, and they perform a valuable function, but there is little room in press relations for the carnival approach that many of them still employ.

Not all bad press relations practices, however, stem from a lack of journalistic background. Many of today's

13

publicity men are ex-newspapermen who, much to the chagrin of their former confreres, repeatedly make the very mistakes they themselves had scorned.

A newspaper career does not automatically qualify one for a responsible position in publicity or public relations. In fact, it is becoming more and more apparent that some of the most inept publicity men are right out of the field of journalism. The idea that a former newspaperman can automatically do a good publicity job is one more manifestation of management's lack of understanding of the job itself. In the first place, not every newspaperman can write. In fact, very few get a chance to write on a consistent basis. Former newspapermen do not have unusual "pull" with papers, particularly the last one they worked on, and what pull they do have is usually good for one time only.

What former newspapermen do have, however, is a working and intimate knowledge of the journalist's role on the newspaper, and they should, consequently, be able to service them well.

The unique pressures attending any press relations job (an occupational hazard) must also share some of the responsibility for the lack of rapport between the press and the publicist. A boss who harries his publicity man, usually out of ignorance of what the job really entails is a strongly contributing factor to poor judgment on the part of the publicity man. "My boss pressured me into pushing too hard," is a common lament.

Pressure, particularly by the small company or client, can make a press relations job a real ulcer alley. Even today, when public relations is enjoying what amounts to a vogue, with all its ramifications explored by educators and practised by leading corporations, an overwhelming number of organizations still think that press publicity is the whole job. Many leading executives who should know better measure the success of their company's entire public relations program by the column inch of press publicity.

Despite these problems, however, there is little justification for the sloppy and unprofessional job being performed today by publicity men in general. This is not only an opinion reached by the authors, after considerable research, but, most important of all, it is the consensus of working newspapermen across the U.S.A. For every real "pro" turning out a workmanlike job, there are many dozens of others making every mistake in the book to the detriment of the publicity business as a whole.

The purpose of this book is neither to indict the publicist (amateur or professional), nor to run interference for the working press (which manages very well without our help). Rather, it is designed to lay down publicity-handling principles which bear in mind both the publicity man's objectives and the newspaper's point of view.

A more widespread understanding and acceptance of such principles is important for two reasons:

On the one hand, newspapers are being subjected to steadily increasing pressure-for-space from outside special interests, and,

On the other hand (but to a lesser degree), newspapers are beginning to regard such outside interests as a source of solid, genuine news. This last is a relatively new development, since the publicity business is a comparative newcomer which, like Topsy, has "just growed."

In its beginnings, publicity was frowned upon by responsible corporations and looked upon with a fishy eye by newspapermen. For years it seemed to belong solely to the press agent and his repertoire of gimmicks, stunts, and hoaxes. Today, a relatively short time later, publicity plays an important role in almost every aspect of professional and non-professional life. Publicity today is the strong right arm of public relations and the unexpected ally of the newspaper business.

Unfortunately, however, in the newpaperman's view, it is an ally to be tolerated, but hardly respected. One major reason for this lack of respect (and in many cases, downright hostility on the part of the newsman is that for years the publicity man has sought the understanding and cooperation of the newspaper without ever taking the pains to understand the newspaper's problems or requirements . . . the very essentials of journalism. This, in effect, has made their relationship a one-way street. This is a point we have attempted to underscore throughout this book in the words of the newspapermen themselves.

Finally, this is not a book on journalism; rather it is a book on how to work with the journalist.

We have not been content to dismiss the city editor with "handle as though he were a Dresden doll," (he's not), or the woman's page editor with, "a lunch is the best way to know her," (it isn't). Instead, we have outlined in detail those basic publicity techniques and journalistic practices that are necessary to obtain publicity coverage. We have done this step by step, department by department, editor by editor.

We do not pretend that ours is the last word on the subject. There are excellent books on public relations and publicity too numerous to list here. Our efforts, however, have been directed toward giving the reader a rare insight into the thinking of the newspaperman himself, through his ideas, his words, and his personal philosophy.

2

A HISTORY
OF NEWSPAPERING

THE DAILY NEWSPAPER, with its accounts of world events, local happenings, features, columns and comics, is as much a part of American life as the morning cup of coffee or the evening meal. We turn to the printed page for our news and often our views, and the voice that speaks from that printed page is a powerful one: It has toppled tyrants, destroyed dictators, stirred patriots and started revolutions. In ruthless hands, it has subjugated whole nations; in the free American society, it is regarded as one of the most potent and important instruments of democracy.

The printed word was recognized as a powerful social force long before the early 19th century when the newspaper business was formally acknowledged as "the fourth estate." In the England and France of the early 1800's, there were three "estates of the realm"—the church, the nobility and the common people. In 1830, Thomas Macaulay, noted English man of letters, observed in *The Edinburgh Review*, "The gallery in which the reporters sit has become a fourth estate of the realm." Today, with the growth and growing prominence of the business of public relations and publicity, some practitioners in this field like to think of themselves as members of "the fifth estate," and many people both inside and outside the business regard it as something of a Twentieth Century phenomenon.

In reality, of course, there is nothing recent or new about the business at all. The desire of one group of human beings to let other human beings know what they're doing is as old as the desire of all human beings to know what's going on in the first place. News and publicity have come hand in hand from the mists of antiquity, and the paths of ancient history are littered with the evidence.

Forty-four hundred years ago, for instance, the newsmen of Ur and Uruk in Mesopotamia were reporting on price controls, business regulations and other general news of the day. Their stories were published on clay tablets which, though they may not have enjoyed the large circulations of today's newspapers, were certainly a lot more durable.

In 351 B. C., according to Demosthenes, a statesman of no small stature in Athens, the Athenians wandered through the streets of their city inquiring of one another, "What is the news?" The walls of Pompeii were covered with election appeals and scribbled inscriptions giving the passing reader the gossip, scandals and politics of the day. And China was publishing metropolitan gazettes as early as the first centuries after Christ, although Gutenberg didn't get around to inventing movable types until the 15th century.

As the news business grew, so did the publicity business. The old Egyptian, Persian and Assyrian rulers, for example, apparently had their own press agents, for practically everything known about them today was found in what remains of efforts to publicize and glorify them.

Statues, monuments, pyramids and tombs were among the various media by which the ancients let the man on the street know just what a bargain they were getting in the king line. Two remaining samples, the great Egyptian obelisks known as "Cleopatra's Needles," are fairly substantial (200 tons each) examples of "puff"—unadulterated, out-and-out publicity. These 69-foot items were erected by one Thothmes III in about 1460 at Heliopolis, where Moses grew up. The heiroglyphics were engraved several inches deep to make certain they would last, and their (to date) deathless prose, reading from top to bottom, tells (on the middle columns) what a great king was Thothmes III, and (on the side columns) what a great fellow was Rameses II.

In later centuries, in England, kings maintained Lords Chancellor as "keepers of the King's Conscience," whose job it was to keep news of the king's munificence and bravery flowing from the king to the people, especially in election years.

But kings didn't have the publicity field to themselves. During the days when knighthood was in flower, a really big wheel in the knight business would have his own "avant courier," literally, a man who ran before, to let everyone know that the great and famous dragonslayer Sir This or That was on his way.

The invention of movable types and subsequent mechanical inventions did not put the spoken word out of business. In old England, the news of the day was relayed by strolling minstrels who sang merry little ballads about the latest hanging, death of a king, or strangling in Lancashire. Even in the early years of this century, the spoken word served to relay the printed word. In a small coal-mining village in Scotland, for instance, it was the nightly custom for the miners and their families to gather under the gas lamp in the square to listen as the only villager who could read, read aloud the day's paper to them.

The colonists who came to America were steeped in the tradition of British journalism which was rather drab and ultraconservative. The first newspaper was probably *The Oxford Gazette,* a semi-weekly single sheet (soon renamed *The London Gazette*) which was printed in 1665. The term "newspaper," however, did not come into being until five years later. Ever since the first printing press had been set up in England in 1476, printing and discussion had been under strict governmental regulation in England, and when the colonists began their publishing ventures, those strictures were extended across the Atlantic.

The first printing press had arrived in the Colonies in 1638, but for lack of type and printers, it lay rusting for 16 years until it fell to Harvard University and began that institution's long publishing career. Even then, the newspaper business did not quickly take root in the otherwise fertile soil of the New World.

Instead, the Colonists contented themselves with the printing of Bibles, psalmbooks, tracts, pamphlets and primers, but no one bothered with newspapers. For one thing, the governors of the Colonies felt that printing was dangerous and there were those government restraints on publishing. For another, the early American communities were small, isolated and very busy, and the coffee houses and wayside conversations seemed to provide enough exchange of news to satisfy everyone.

A few English newspapers, arriving by boat, were circulated, but it wasn't until 1690 that anything that could properly be called a newspaper was published in America.

This was called *"Publick Occurrences Both Forreign and Domestick,"* and its publisher was Benjamin Harris who ran a coffee house and, therefore, naturally knew what a valuable commodity news could be. Ever since the first coffee house had opened in Constantinople in 1554, these comfortable conversation spots had become centers for the spreading of news and political gossip in all countries.

Each coffee house, like each newspaper today, attracted its own particular patrons, and a merchant who wanted to keep up with the market and current events spent several hours a day literally drinking in the news of the day.

Benjamin Harris, however, had not always been just a coffee house proprietor. He had formerly been a London bookseller and publisher. Unfortunately, a pamphlet he had published had been considered seditious by the British government which promptly jailed him. As soon as his imprisonment was over, Harris had fled to America.

His very first edition of *"Publick Occurrences Etc."* landed him in hot water with the authorities once more. It was a newsy, three-page paper (the fourth page was left blank for private correspondence) and the publisher was absolutely impartial in his criticism of both sides in the French and Indian War. He accused the French king of immorality, and criticised the British allies, the Mohawk Indians, for their savage treatment of French prisoners.

21

The governor and council of the Massachusetts Bay Colony listened with a tin ear to such free and unvarnished speech. Although in Issue No. I, Harris had announced that his newspaper would be "furnished once a moneth (or if any Glut of Occurrences happen oftener) " *Publick Occurrences* never saw another issue. It was suppressed by the Governor four days after it appeared, and it was fully 14 years before anyone tried again to publish a newspaper in the Colonies.

The next newspaper fared better, primarily because its publisher, John Campbell, knew which side his type was inked on. Campbell was the Colony postmaster and he took great pains to stay within the bounds of what the governor and his council regarded as propriety. *The Boston News-Letter,* started by Campbell in 1704, became the country's first continously published newspaper. (It flourished right up to the Revolution, and then, since it was a Tory publication, it suspended shortly before the British evacuated Boston.)

In 1719, 15 years after the *News-Letter* was started, publisher Campbell lost his postmastership to William Brooker, who naturally expected to take over the publishing venture as well. Campbell, however, was most unsporting about the matter and refused to give up his newspaper. So the new postmaster started one of his own.

To print his *Boston Gazette,* Brooker hired one James Franklin, whose apprentice was his 13-year-old brother, Ben. For the next two years, Franklin, Brooker and the *Gazette* prospered together. Then, in 1721, Brooker lost both his postmaster's job and his newspaper, and the new publisher took the printing of the *Gazette* to another shop.

In what was beginning to become a pattern, James

Franklin, now without his primary source of revenue, started *his* own newspaper. His *New England Courant* lasted a lively five-and-a-half years. It was so lively, in fact, that the Massachusetts council had banned James Franklin as a publisher, and he had put his brother, Benjamin, in as nominal publisher.

The younger Franklin was so shabbily treated by his older brother, however, that he finally ran away to Philadelphia which already had two newspapers of its own—*The American Weekly Mercury* started only one day later than the *Boston Gazette* in 1719, and a newspaper begun by one Samuel Keimer in 1728, who saddled it with the improbable name: *The Universal Instructor in All Arts and Sciences, and Pennsylvania Gazette.*

Young Ben Franklin began writing essays known as "The Busy-Body Papers" for Keimer's newspaper and did so well and so thriftily that in 1729 he bought out the publisher. He lopped off the first half of the newspaper's name and was so successful with the second half, *The Pennsylvania Gazette,* that he was able to retire at the age of 42.

In the meantime, New York had acquired its first newspaper. *The New-York Gazette* was founded in 1725 by William Bradford, a Philadelphia printer who had introduced printing into Pennsylvania and then had moved his plant to New York. (It was Bradford's son, Andrew, who had started Philadelphia's *American Weekly Mercury.*) Bradford's paper was strictly a mouthpiece for the government of the New York colony, and in 1733, leaders of the opposition to Governor William Cosby persuaded John Peter Zenger, a printer, to start a competing newspaper. When Zenger accepted the challenge, he earmarked his place in history.

Zenger had been apprenticed to Bradford eight years, becoming a freeman of New York City in 1723. In 1733, he was known for having published the first arithmetic textbook printed in this country. Today his name is virtually synonymous with "freedom of the press."

Zenger began publication of his *New-York Weekly Journal* on Nov. 5, 1733. During the year that followed, his paper was greatly responsible for rousing public opinion against the government of the colony. It carried squibs, lampoons and satirical ballads, contributed by some of the finest minds in the city, and all aimed at the administration. On Nov. 17, 1734, Zenger was arrested and tossed into prison on grounds of having published seditious libels when he printed statements to the effect that the governor was interfering with the process of law in the courts.

On Jan. 28, 1735, although the grand jury had found no bill aaginst Zenger, the attorney general filed an information charging him with "false, scandalous, malicious and seditious libels." By the time the trial began, Zenger had already been imprisoned for ten months.

One of the first moves made on behalf of the administration was to deprive Zenger of counsel. Zenger's lawyers, James Alexander and William Smith, two of New York's most eminent attorneys, were found by Chief Justice William de Lancey to be in contempt of court, and they were denied the right to represent their client.

Secretly they went to Andrew Hamilton, a Philadelphia lawyer famous for his learning and eloquence, and persuaded him to defend Zenger. Hamilton's dramatic and unexpected appearance in court on the first day of the trial created a sensation. His masterly argument in

24

defense of Zenger created the great legal precedent for freedom of the press.

The question at issue in the Zenger trial was the definition of the word "libel." Hamilton's argument was based on the truth contained in the statements said to be libelous. The jury chose Hamilton's rather than the state's definition, and found Zenger "not guilty."

His acquittal in August, 1733 is regarded as the first great victory for freedom of the press—not only in the colonies, but throughout the British Empire and the United States as well. The Hamiltonian doctrine—that the evidence of the truth of statements published with good intentions may be introduced by the defense in a criminal libel suit—later became a part of most state constitutions.

By the middle of the 18th century, there were a number of other publications going strong in Maryland, Rhode Island, the Carolinas, New Hampshire, Georgia, New Jersey, Delaware, East-Florida, Vermont and Maine.

The newspapers of the day were weeklies, measuring about 11 x 15 inches and carrying about four pages of news with extra pages added to accommodate advertising. All of them were well patronized by advertisers, and the ad pages looked something like today's classified ad sections.

There were no editorial pages, but plenty of editorial comment. This was sprinkled liberally through the news columns—a practice that persisted in small town weeklies up to the beginning of the Twentieth Century.

There was practically no local news, since there were no local reporters, and editors regarded news primarily as a record of history. The custom was that the editor would cover any news of first-rate importance that took place in his own neighborhood for his own paper, then other newspapers clipped it. Thus, the colonial papers had a sort of informal cooperative going for themselves —something like today's Associated Press.

For other news sources, the editors turned to newspapers from England, letters from other cities or from England, word-of-mouth reports by ship captains, post riders and travelers. The news was padded out with dissertations on politics and economics, satirical essays on social customs, poems and other literary efforts.

With the coming of the Revolution, the English papers were cut off altogether as a source of news. It was at this time, too, that public relations began to be a force in the colonies, developing as various power groups and special interest groups found they needed to rally public support to their causes.

Much as Printer Zenger had aroused public opinion against corrupt colonial government through his newspaper, the spokesmen for a free and independent America roused support for the Revolutionary cause through the newspapers. The printed word was a powerful extension of the spoken word, and was used liberally and well by such "agitators" as Tom Paine, Benjamin Franklin, Thomas Jefferson, Patrick Henry.

It was not until after the Revolution that the first daily newspapers made their appearance on the American scene. They came into existence not so much because editors were burning to provide their readers with timely news, but because the publishers had to meet the competition of the coffee houses.

Just as soon as ships arrived in the harbors of Philadelphia and New York, bulletins were posted in the coffee houses, giving the merchants reports of the offerings of importers. Since this kind of news was one of the chief reasons merchants bought newspapers, the editors and publishers felt the pinch of the competition. *The Pennsylvania Evening Post,* established as a tri-weekly, went daily in 1783, and *The Pennsylvania Packet and Daily Advertiser* followed suit a year later.

But it was *The New York Daily Advertiser,* founded in 1785 by Francis Childs, which was the first American paper to be founded as a daily. By the end of the 18th century, the political papers also had adopted daily publication.

This was an era of ardent partisanship in journalism, and the journalistic obligation to report the news fully, fairly and accurately barely lived through it. From the time of George Washington's second term until after the Civil War, newspapers took sides loudly and vehemently and in every news story. Both business papers and those papers established solely to represent one political point of view were guilty of printing slanted and distorted news and personal abuse. There were assaults and duels among editors of the time, and there was widespread villification of public and political figures.

For example, when President Abraham Lincoln was en route to Washington for his inaugural, a planned assassination attempt was foiled by removing the president from the train taking him to the capital. Frank Leslie's *Illustrated Press* in New York, reporting the story, commented that if Lincoln had really wanted to serve his country, he would have remained on the train and let himself be killed.

Although fair and unbiased press was definitely in the minority, not all newspapers were tainted with the ugly partisanship of the day. Noah Webster, who later made a name for himself as a man of many words and made "Webster" a synonym for "dictionary" founded *The American Minerva* in New York in 1793 as a voice for the Federalist party. Four years later, it took the name *Commercial Advertiser* and published under that name for more than 100 years.

The National Intelligencer, established in Washington in 1800 by Samuel Harrison Smith, was only mildly partisan and quite reliable in its reporting of news. It was for many years considered "the" authority on Washington news, but it was displaced as a spokesman for the government when Andrew Jackson became president. *The United States Telegraph,* founded by Duff Green in 1825, became Jackson's first Washington paper, to be supplanted in 1830 by the *Washington Globe.*

The American Citizen of the early 1800's was a vicious organ of the George Clinton faction of the Democratic party. To oppose it, Alexander Hamilton and his friends organized a stock company and in 1801 founded the *New York Evening Post.* In 1829, William Cullen Bryant became the editor, and held that post until his death in 1878.

The Penny Papers

The first real step toward the modern concept of newspapering came in the 1830's when "the penny papers" appeared on the publishing scene. These were smaller in size and they cost only a penny instead of the six cents charged by the larger papers.

The most startling innovation of these new newspapers was that they preferred printing news to supporting a political party or a mercantile class. They featured human interest stories and local news, and were geared

28

to talk to people on the lower social and economic levels. They talked so successfully that they quickly built up large circulations and large advertising revenues which enabled them to improve their news services and install fast cylinder presses. The penny papers were the leaders in the use of the expresses and telegraph for transmitting news quickly, and their emphasis on local news and timeliness marked the beginning of modern journalism.

The New York Sun, founded in 1833, was the first successful penny daily. The New York Herald, founded by James Gordon Bennett, followed two years later. The Philadelphia Public Ledger and the Baltimore Sun were founded in 1836 and 1837 by three New York printers.

Horace Greeley founded The New York Tribune as a penny paper in 1841, and The New York Times was started as a penny paper in 1851, by Henry J. Raymond, George Jones and Edward B. Wesley. All but the Sun soon went to two cents, enlarged their size and scope. Bennett and Greeley were rival editors for thirty years, both dying in 1872. They were the leading figures in an era of personal journalism. Greeley was an idealist, and his newspaper reflected his wildly varying interests and causes. It was Bennett who sent Stanley to find Livingston, and introduced financial and society departments as part of the daily paper.

In 1855, The New York Daily News (no relation to the present newspaper) was founded as a penny paper and an organ of Tammany Hall. During the Civil War, it came into the hands of Benjamin Wood, brother of Fernando Wood, the New York Mayor. Both were ardently pro-slavery.

In fact, the paper was so loudly pro-slavery that a

combined military and postal blockade forced it to close down for 18 months in 1861 and 1862.

After the Civil War, *The News* built up a large circulation in the tenement house districts, peddling exposes and sensations. It was a successful business undertaking, remaining in the family until Wood's death in 1900. The following year, Frank A. Munsey bought *The News* from Wood's widow for $340,000. Munsey wrought remarkable improvements in *The News*—cleaned it up, tempered its sensationalism, improved its news quality. In fact he improved the paper so much that it lost its public and perished in 1906.

These were the days of color and personality in the newspaper and the days when the popular concept of the newspaperman as an adventurer and jack-of-all-trades took form. Shortly before the California gold rush, for instance, San Francisco newsmen had to meet three qualifications if they were to succeed: They had to be "true with the rifle, ready with the pen, and quick at the typecase." A reporter applying for a job on a Nevada newspaper in 1874 was asked only one question: "Can you shoot?"

Pioneer newspapers in Kansas found themselves embroiled in the free-state war of 1855, and the staff of the *Lawrence Herald* of Freedom, Kansas, came to work one morning to find the office destroyed by the pro-slavery faction. In retaliation, the *Herald* gave its type to be moulded into the cannonballs used for the attack on Fort Titus. Every discharge of the anti-slavery cannon was called a "new edition" of the *Herald*.

It was after the Civil War that a new concept of the role of the newspaper began to bring about changes in the content of the newspapers of the day. They became more and more independent of party control. By 1880, a fourth of all American newspapers were listed as independent; by 1890, the independents made up one third.

News, not opinion, became the important commodity, and Charles A. Dana of the *New York Sun* told his reporters to "get the news, get all the news, and nothing but the news."

William F. Storey, editor of the *Chicago Times* in 1861 told his reporters that "it is the newspaper's duty to print the news and raise hell."

The definitions of news were as various as the editors who made them, but the point they made was the same. One editor defined news as "anything that will make a woman gasp," but it was John Bogart, city editor of the *New York Sun,* who, in 1800, made the now-classic definition: "If a man bites a dog, that's news."

Important newspapers were also developing outside of New York. *The Chicago Times* was a successful sensation paper after the Civil War. During the war, it had made so many attacks on the union army that General A. E. Burnside seized and suspended it for three days. He rescinded his order only at the request of President Lincoln.

The Times flourished until *The Chicago Tribune* came to control the Chicago newspaper picture. *The Tribune,* founded in 1847, had a hard time until 1855 when Joseph Medill and five partners took it over and made it a strong and successful newspaper.

During the 1870's, *The New York Sun* climbed steadily in prestige and influence. Purchased in 1868 by Charles A. Dana, it became one of the best written and best edited papers in the country. It was sassy and bright and independent of politics, and its human interest stories of New York became one of its chief attractions. But it was Joseph Pulitzer, a Hungarian-born immigrant, who probably did more than any other newspaper man to set the pattern of modern journalism. He had made a success of the *St. Louis Post-Dispatch* and then in 1883 bought *The New York World,* setting the New York newspaper situation on its ear.

The World had been founded as a religious daily in 1860, became moderately successful under the control of Manton Marble in 1869, and then began to slide after it came under the control of Thomas A. Scott of the Pennsylvania Railroad in 1876. Scott unloaded it on Jay Gould in connection with a railroad deal, and by the time Pulitzer bought it in 1883, it was losing $40,000 a year.

Pulitzer turned it into the country's most successful newspaper and by 1887, it had become the most profitable paper ever published.

It was Pulitzer and his *World* that inadvertently led the way to "yellow journalism" and thus to today's newspaper techniques: The use of banner heads, lots of pictures, crusading for popular causes, and the Sunday supplement complete with colored comics.

It was a comic strip, in fact, that gave the name, "yellow journalism" to the kind of newspapering that grew out of the competition between Pulitzer's *World* and *The Journal* of William Randolph Hearst.

After successfully managing *The San Francisco Examiner* in California, Hearst went to New York in 1895 and bought *The Journal* with which to challenge *The World's* supremacy in the city. He brought some of his staff from San Francisco, but he also hired many staffers away from *The World.* One of these was Richard F. Outcault who drew a comic picture series called "The Yellow Kid." When he and "The Kid" went to the Sunday *Journal,* Pulitzer ordered George B. Luks to continue drawing the strip for *The World.*

Thus there were two papers running "The Yellow Kid," and before long, the efforts of both papers to outdo one another in sensationalism, scare heads, and Sunday features became known as "yellow" journalism. Many newspapers in other cities followed suit. One of the phenomena of this era was the promotion of the Spanish-American war through hysterical propaganda against Spain, based on exposures of Spanish atrocities in Cuba. *The Journal* and *The World* were by no means alone in their hysteria, but they were the leaders in it.

The all-out competition between the two papers developed large circulations for both and affected the journalistic practices of city papers throughout the country. The jaundice did not begin to fade until shortly after the turn of the century when *The World* gradually retired from the competition and *The New York Times* began to rise in power, prestige and circulation.

Indirectly, *The Times* may owe its present prestige to yellow journalism. Adolph S. Ochs, publisher of *The Chatanooga* (Tenn.) *Times* and taken over *The New York Times* in 1896 when it was failing, reducing its price to a penny two years later. When the Pulitzer-Hearst competition broke out like yellow fever, Ochs chose to compete by going in the opposite direction.

While *The World* and *The Journal* knocked each other's brains out with scandals and exposes of the most sensational sort, *The New York Times* announced it would carry only "All the news that's fit to print."

33

And while Hearst and Pulitzer poured printer's ink by the bucket into bold, black, banners, *The Times* confined itself to dignified one-column headlines and commented in an ironic motto: "It does not soil the breakfast cloth."

At the turn of the 19th century, other important newspapers were founded across the country. *The Denver Post,* founded in 1892, was bought three years later by Fred G. Bonfils and Harry H. Tammen, and came to prominence as a "yellow" paper with policies that were not really modified until after World War II when Palmer Hoyt became its publisher.

William Allen White bought *The Emporia* (Kansas) *Gazette* when it was five years old in 1895, and made it nationally famous through his editorial writings. In 1908, Mary Baker Eddy established *The Christian Science Monitor,* a good-looking and high-minded newspaper that fought yellow journalism and emphasized international news.

The Twentieth Century and the tabloid newspaper were born the same day.

On January 1, 1900, the first experimental tabloid issue of *The New York World* appeared. It was designed, edited and christened by its father, Alfred Harmsworth (Viscount Northcliffe), a British journalist and newspaper proprietor who had founded the *London Daily Mail* four years earlier. *The Mail* was the first halfpenny morning paper to succeed in a big scale in England, and its publisher had freely borrowed many American newspaper techniques to bring this about. He was a frequent visitor to the United States, and it was when he was put in charge of *The New York World* for one day that the tabloid was born.

The newspaper that appeared on New York's news-stands that cold New Year's Day set the pattern for all the tabloids that followed, and marked the first—and some say, the last—journalistic innovation of the century. It is common to think of a tabloid newspaper merely as one with a small page size, convenient for reading on buses and subways or crowded apartments. If this were true, all the earliest American newspapers would have qualified as tabloids. However, the most distinctive characteristics of a tabloid go beyond its page size—which is the folded-in-half size of the normal eight-column paper. Tabloid newspapering is a style and an approach distinguished primarily by an extensive use of pictures and a condensed and lively presentation of the news.

Lord Northcliffe started his own tabloid, *The Daily Mirror*, in London in 1903, but it was not until 1919 that the first tabloid hit the newsstands in America. There were 17 other newspapers being published in New York when Robert R. McCormick and Joseph Medill Patterson, grandsons of Joseph Medill, launched *The Illustrated Daily News*. Within six years it had won a circulation of 1,000,000.

The circulation of the upstart newspaper grew, in no small measure, from the sensationalism of its news pages, and brought it into direct competition with Hearst's sensation paper, the morning *American*. So, in 1924, Hearst founded his own tabloid, *The Daily Mirror*, and three months later, Bernarr MacFadden launched the tabloid *Daily Graphic*.

Thus began the "war of the tabs," as the three papers tried to outdo one another. Hearst sold *The Mirror* in 1928, although he had to take it back later. *The Graphic* died in 1932. *The News*, acquiring dignity with success, abandoned much of its sensationalism (but none of its originality) and built up the largest neswpaper circulation in America—around 2,000,000 daily, and 3,000,000 Sundays, when last counted.

The success of *The News* has prompted other publishers to try the tabloid form, and in 1960 there were 45 tabloid papers published across the country. Some of the best known are the *Rocky Mountain News* in Denver, *The Chicago Sun-Times*, *The Philadelphia News*, and *The Washington News*.

In the century since the Civil War, two factors, chains and consolidations, have wrought great changes in the newspaper scene. Edward W. Scripps evolved the formula for newspaper chains, and his 34 newspapers across the country earned him the first fortune in chain newspapers. It was Scripps' practice to establish papers in medium-size cities with cheap equipment, put young men from his organization in charge with working partnerships, sells his papers for a penny a copy, and campaign for causes that were popular among the common people. In 1922, Scripps retired and turned his properties over to his son, Robert, who formed an organization known as Scripps-Howard. Howard was Roy W. Howard who had been general manager of the United Press, founded in 1907 as a news-gathering agency for Scripps.

William Randolph Hearst enlarged the chain idea, starting with the *San Francisco Examiner, New York Journal*, and *Evening Journal*. Altogether, he bought or established more than 40 newspapers.

The newspaper chain idea may have meant more newspapers under the control of one company, but at least it produced more newspapers. Consolidation, a recognized technique for cleaning up the competition, has, on the other hand, resulted in fewer newspapers. There is an increasing number of cities with one-newspaper ownership. There were 2,461 dailies in the United States in 1916. By 1960, there were only 1,766. Some towns may have two papers, but both are owned by the same man or company.

While the number of newspapers is decreasing, newspaper circulations are increasing, and in 1960, newspapers found their way into the homes of 88 percent of all U. S. families.

The dangers inherent in such a situation—more and more people reading newspapers representing fewer and fewer points of view—is offset to some degree by the competition of other media—magazines, radio and television. Will Rogers' quizzical comment of the Twenties, "all I know is what I read in the papers," is no longer true. The television debates of the 1961 presidential campaign provided dramatic evidence that newspapers are no longer alone in informing or in swaying public opinion.

Moreover, readers, listeners and viewers are now getting their news with a greater seasoning of interpretation through commentators, columnists and special article writers. Any social action taken by the people of the United States is a direct reflection of all these efforts.

Now that television has become a potent communicating media, it will have to share increasingly in the steady stream of criticism that has kept the United States press on its toes ever since the first issue of *Publick Occurrences.* This criticism has ranged from the sober concern of responsible and scholarly citizens to the angry, partisan and generally accurate sniping of a TV personality.

But whatever form it takes, the criticism is healthy, for The Press is still the most powerful voice in the land, and republics are still dedicated to the principle that informed citizens will make the right decisions—at least, most of the time.

3

PUTTING THE PAPER TOGETHER

OF ALL FIELDS of endeavor in the United States, the newspaper business is probably one of the most popular, over-glamorized and least understood.

Well-read, well-educated and intelligent people still refer to a feature story as a "column" and to a news item as "ad." Many still offer to pay to have some bit of news printed, and others call up to order headlines and dictate word for word the story they wish to see in print.

People of gentle mien and kind hearts want to know why it is necesary to print news that is sad, horrifying or sordid, and feel that the newspaper owes a responsibility to the public to report also on the "good" things (the things which, incidentally, usually don't make news).

In many communities it is still felt that the appearance of one's name in the public prints is a blot on the family 'scutcheon, while other citizens assume that since they pay the dime or the nickel, they thereby own the right to dictate the paper's policies and stories.

A large body of readers feel that the newspaper is— or ought to be—a public service, bound by principle if not by law to take up the cudgels for Right and Good causes, to expose corruption in high places, and to omit from its pages all informational matter that is not uplifting or educational. Others see the newspaper as purely an advertising medium and cynically consider its news columns to be bought and sold as well as the advertising —using pressure and influence instead of money as the medium of exchange.

To the non-professional man or woman who is tagged "publicity chairman" for the Parent-Teacher Association or Junior Chamber of Commerce, the newspaper is a bewildering and formidable force, sometimes a friend, sometimes an unfathomable "enemy." Who can understand why the paper did not send a photographer to cover the election of officers, but gave several columns of space to a cute picture of a boy and his dog?

Sometimes, if the newspaper reporters have time and the publicity chairman has faith, the mysteries of newspapering will slowly unravel, and after a year, the publicity chairman will be a pretty good editorial assistant. More often, however, the newspaperman is too rushed to conduct a short course in journalism, and the publicity chairman is too frustrated to care.

To the professional publicity man, the newspaper is one thing—his reason for being. Since his sole function is to get into print news of some special interest, the newspaper is the very lifeblood of his occupation.

Some publicity men reason—and with some validity —that their work is an important adjunct of the newspaper business. Publicity representatives do, in fact, provide the newspapers of today with considerable important material. When the publicity is handled by what newspapermen like to call "a real pro," the relationship is a good one, with professional respect on both sides. When the job is mishandled, one more log is tossed on the smouldering fires of distrust which most newspapermen harbor toward publicity men.

Few publicity men, however, take the trouble to really learn the newspaper business, contenting themselves with dealing with a select group of newspapermen. They work on the surface, concentrating solely on the "who" of the paper rather than on the "how" and the "why." It is this lack of understanding and interest on the part of people who actually are in a quasi-newspaper business that marks most publicity men as parasites in the eyes of most newspaper people.

Even the publicity man who likes to think of himself as the good right arm, the "extra reporter," "the middle man" or "the fifth estate," is usually as ignorant of the workings of the newspaper as is the layman who only reads it.

Plays, novels, movies, and comic strips have helped to widen the gap between the newspaper and the people to whom it talks by cloaking the business of newspapering in an aura of glamor, excitement, danger—and sometimes mystery. Newspaper men and women themselves have contributed to the artificial picture—often deliberately, out of vanity, but more often out of the pressures of deadlines and the city desk which do not allow time to explain, to be patient, or to show much regard for the feelings of others.

This kind of ignorance of what a newspaper is and stands for, of what reporters are and do, has always been a matter for concern in a republic founded upon an enlightened electorate. In the larger world and quieter times of yesterday, it was a condition that could wait. But in an age when science has widened the world's horizons and shrunk its boundaries, no citizen ought to be ignorant of the workings of what is still the most profound influence upon public opinion—the local newspaper.

41

There are immediate, practical reasons, too, why people should know what goes on inside the newspaper plant. Today, more and more, the average citizen whose grandmother never saw her name in print except on the occasion of her marriage, finds himself dealing daily and directly with the local newspaper. Sometimes it is on his own behalf—his business or his family; sometimes it is on behalf of the community. Women's clubs are increasingly active and increasingly publicity-consicious, and so also are the men's service organizations like Kiwanis and Rotary and Lions. The manager or owner of a small firm or modest factory often finds himself called upon to perform the functions of a trained publicist with neither the training nor the time to acquire the necessary skills and understanding.

Not everyone can—or needs to—attend journalism school to understand the newspaper business, but everyone should have a working knowledge of how the newspaper functions and why it functions. Such knowledge is not simply an essential for the professional and amateur publicist, but it can make the average newspaper buyer a more aware and more critical reader.

The confusion about the newspaper's role in society —it is a business or a profession?—is not limited to the millions not engaged in the newspaper business. It is a subject for debate among the people in the business themselves, and probably has been from the date of publication of the first news sheet—a clay tablet lost somewhere in time. In various ages and in different places, the question has been answered sometimes one way, sometimes the other.

The truth is that there is a distinctly schizophrenic quality about any successful newspaper venture. It is—

and it must be—both a business and a profession, and it must maintain a careful balance between the two facets of its personality if it is to succeed. Newspaper graveyards are filled with the remains of newspapers which earned acclaim for fine editorial tradition, yet were doomed by a clumsy business operation. And there are just as many dead papers which became so much the catspaws of their business departments that they lost their editorial lives.

A simplified summation of the age-old argument might be this: Business men run newspapers; professionals work on them.

Every newspaper, whether it is *The Hobart* (Ind.) *Gazette,* which comes out once a week, or *The New York Daily News,* which publishes five editions a day, is organized into the same three departments: Editorial, mechanical, and business.

No paper can operate with fewer than these. Every paper has to have a news-gathering department (editorial) , the news has to be set in type and printed (mechanical) , and somebody has to pay the bills (business) .

(On some newspapers, advertising and circulation are separate divisions, but in any case, they are a part of the over-all business operation.)

Generally, the organization of a newpaper breaks down like this:

Editorial

Top men in the editorial department are the executive editors, the editorial writers and department editors.

Working under their direction are the city room (or local room) , the telegraph or cable editor, and the photographers.

43

The art department, morgue and library are vital to the editorial operation.

Mechanical

The composing room, engraving division and the stereotyping department turn the news-gathering work of editorial into a tangible product—the newspaper.

The press room then turns this product out in quantity, and the mailing division (sometimes allied with the circulation department) gets the product ready for distribution to the readers.

Business

Within the business department come the newspaper's administrative heads, the circulation division and auditing division. Circulation is a key operation. There is nothing more useless than a newpaper that cannot get out to be read.

On the next echelon are the advertising division which brings in the revenue, and the promotion division which helps to sell the finished product.

The promotion of newspaper sales is usually the function of the advertising division.

These, therefore, are the three arms of the newspaper. Just how complex these departments may become, and how many people they may employ, will depend upon the size of the newspaper and the town it serves. *The New York Times* has an editorial staff of more than 1,400; *The New York Daily News* has a photo staff of fifty. On a small-town weekly, on the other hand, the publisher may be his own editor, ad man, reporter, and proof reader. His mechanical department—the back shop—

may consist of only a linotype or two, a flatbed press, metal saw, casting box, and a folder. His "staff" may a journeyman printer and an apprentice.

No matter how large the paper or how small, however, the techniques of turning news into newspapers are the same. Only the perspective is different because successful newspapers must mirror the communities in which they function.

Thus in a town of 10,000, the arrest of a drunken gandy-dancer may make news, and a commercial public relations promotion such as a Betty Crocker cooking school may even make Page One. In New York, on the other hand, the gandy-dancer would have to be doing something more bizarre than just getting plastered to accomplish this feat.

An actual tour of a newspaper plant gives the visitor a vivid picture of the physical establishment, but no great comprehension of how or why the newspaper operates as it does. Even big city reporters who have come up through the ranks of copy boys and have never had the all-around experience of a small paper, may be totally ignorant of the mechanics by which a news story becomes a part of the newspaper.

The Editorial Department

Regardless of what you may see on television, reporters, photographers and bawling city editors do not make up the entire staff of a newspaper. On large papers, the editorial staff can include the following positions:

Editor, executive editor, associate editors, managing editor, news editor, city editor, Sunday editor, telegraph editor, wire editor, make-up editor, sports editor, financial editor, labor editor, women's editor, editorial writers, special writers, feature editor;

Picture editor, rotogravure editor, society editor, drama editor, columnists, literary editor, music editor, movie editor, cartoonists, art editor, radio-TV editor, automobile editor, travel editor, religious editor, real estate editor, stamp editor, science editor, aviation editor, garden editor, farm editor, recordings editor;

Copyreaders, rewrite men, reporters, photographers, artists, clerks, office boys, copy boys, messengers.

On a smaller daily, of course, the staff will be proportionately smaller. A newspaper like *The Gary* (Ind.) *Post Tribune,* for instance, with a circulation of 60,000, cannot afford to keep a staff of reporters and photographers in foreign lands or even in Washington, D.C., and at the United Nations. Still, it gives its readers thorough coverage on all the world events of the day by use of the wire services. These services maintain reporters and photographers all over the world, and their stories come directly into the Gary newsroom by way of the Teletype.

Similarly, such a paper could not afford a large staff of artists, cartoonists, special feature writers, and columnists. Yet the paper's readers are supplied with a wide variety of columns of comment, editorial cartoons, and other feature material purchased from outside sources. All of the news and feature material pouring in from these outside sources is correlated with the work of the local staff which gives the city complete coverage of its own current events. The editorial department must also work closely with the advertising department since the amount of advertising sold for the day generally determines the number of pages in the paper, and to some degree determines how many columns an editor will have for news.

Ed. vs Ad.

There is a long-standing and frequently loud competition between editorial and advertising for space in the paper. Advertising is inclined to proclaim loftily that it, after all, pays Editorial's salaries, and if it weren't for Advertising, there would be no paper on which to work. Editorial is quick to point out that it takes circulation to sell ads, and if it weren't for an editorial content that wins readership, Advertising would have nothing to sell to its clients.

Getting an additional page to accommodate extra news or extra advertising presents many mechanical problems and is costly as well as difficult. What usually happens is that news of lesser import is boiled down or tossed out altogether.

When this happens, many a publicity pro or publicity chairman is left standing on a windy street corner vainly thumbing through the paper and wondering how he's going to explain *this* one.

Probably the simplest way to learn and understand how a newspaper is put together is to follow the progress of a news story from the moment it happens until the account of that happening appears in the printed column of the day's papers. The process is the same whether the story concerns a fire, a parade or a meeting of the P.T.A.

The News Tip

The first step in the evolution of any news story is the "tip."

This may be a phone call from a faithful reader or anonymous bystander, a press release from a professional publicity man or publicity chairman of a community organization. It may come over the police radio or from the newspaper's own staff, the beat man who comes upon it in the course of covering his routine assignment.

If the news story is a relatively minor one, the newspaper can usually handle it in the office, just as it stands or by augmenting the information in a release by a phone call to the publicity person who sent it out.

If, however, it is a breaking story such as a four-alarm fire, the city editor will assign a reporter to cover it or to assist the beat man who is already on the job. In the case of a fire or a parade and like stories, photographers also will be assigned to cover.

(Let no one infer, at this point, that we are suggesting that an enterprising publicity man start a four-alarm fire in order to get out the reporters and photographers. There are other ways, equally dramatic and less complicated, to capture the interest and cooperation of a newspaper.)

Reporter Assigned

The reporter is now on his way to the fire with his press card (usually sealed in plastic) plainly visible to get him through police lines and fire lines, a fistful of copy paper for taking notes, a pocketful of sharp pencils, a few dimes or slugs for the telephone, and carfare.

When he arrives at the scene, he probably notes the location of the nearest telephone for future use and then proceeds to get his story, taking such notes as will help him get statements correct, figures accurate. A few re-

PUTTING THE PAPER TOGETHER

The progress of a news story or picture from the moment of its happening to the printed page is one of the most fascinating aspects of the newspaper business— and one that is understood by relatively few outside the business, and not everyone in it. Here, reproduced through the courtesy of *The New York Daily News,* is a series of pictures showing step by step how a news *event* becomes a news *story.*

1. THE TIP AND ASSIGNMENT. It may be a phone call or a press release, but in any case, the tip notifies the city desk (above) that something is happening. It may be a PTA meeting, a parade, or a four-alarm fire. If it's important enough, the city editor assigns a reporter to cover it.

2. PHOTO ASSIGNMENT: The picture editor assigns a photographer to cover the event, giving him the phoned-in information or the photo memo telling him what's happening, where, and who or what to shoot. *The News* has some 50 photographers on tap.

3. REWRITE. If it's a spot news story, the reporter may call in from the scene, and the rewrite man (with headphones) takes the notes and writes the story. Sometimes the reporter returns to the office and writes his own story.

4. RETOUCH. The film, rushed back to the office from the scene, is developed and printed and the photograph goes to the retouch artist who brightens highlights and airbrushes extraneous backgrounds to get the best reproduction possible.

5. LINOTYPE. The story, which may be cut up into several pieces goes to several typesetters who reproduce it in type metal on machines. *The News* has 77 such machines working three shifts to turn out a day's newspaper.

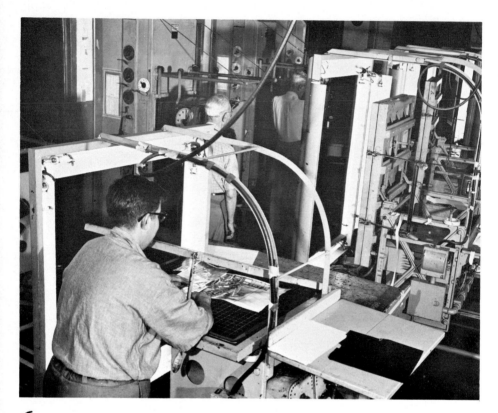

6. PHOTOENGRAVING. The picture is also reproduced in metal. The photoengraver (above) places it
on his copy board, preparing to photograph it through
the screen that will give it the familiar newspaper
"dot" formations.

7. JIGSAW PUZZLE. The story (in metal type), the picture (on metal plates), the ads (composed of both type and plates) are assembled in the form—that metal frame lying on the stone above. The makeup editor, at left, supervises the assembling. The page layout showing what goes where is under the compositor's thumb.

8. ROLLING A MAT. From the assembled page a matrix is made. A special, pliable paper takes and holds a clear impression when it is pressed down on the type metal.

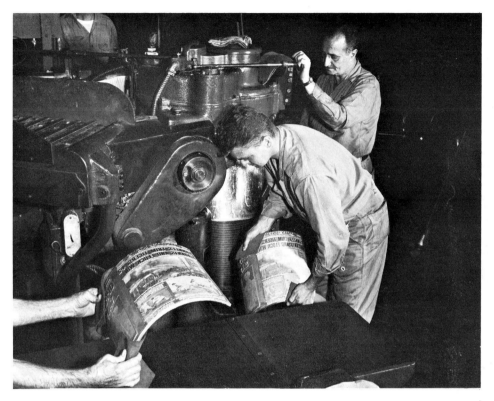

9. STEREO. The "mat," now bent into a semi-cylindrical shape to fit the rotary press, goes to the stereotype foundry. Here it is used to cast a curved metal reproduction of the original flat metal page.

10. LOCK-UP. The curved metal cast is placed on the press, locked firmly into place, then protected by the curved metal cover.

11. THE PRESSES ROLL. Once all casts are locked on, the presses start to roll. The papers come off the press onto the assembly belts assembled, folded, cut and counted. Then its on to the trucks, and off to the newsstands.

porters use shorthand, but most of them have their own brand of scrambled abbreviations. Copious notes don't necessarily produce a good story. ("You're a reporter, not a secretary," one city editor told a zealous beginner.)

With experience, the reporter (who is often called a leg man because his job involves getting around) learns to take his notes in a way that will be easy to dictate on the phone. This is more easily done when he's covering a speech than in the midst of a four-alarm fire, but it can be done.

The Story Is Filed

Once the reporter has all the information he needs or can get up to the moment, he files his story. On an out-of-town assignment, he would send it by wire. On local assignments, he uses the telephone. Occasionally, if he has all the information he needs, he will come back to the office and write the story himself.

Not all reporters, however, are the best writers, just as not all rewrite men are the best leg men. So the man on the beat or the reporter assigned usually gives his story to a rewrite man.

The Rewrite Man Takes Over

When the man on the story calls the city desk to say he has it, the deskman turns the call over to the rewrite man. A few exceptional reporters can dictate a story word for word as it probably will appear in print, but in most cases it is the rewrite man who takes the reporter's information and impressions and turns them into vivid, story-telling prose.

He may write the story in the general form the re-

49

porter gives it, or he may rearrange it for better effect. Sometimes he takes notes; sometimes he writes the story directly on the typewriter. On large newspapers, he has a head-set; on smaller papers, a crick in the neck from holding the phone between his ear and his shoulder.

Taking news on the telephone is his primary job, but a rewrite man is also often called upon to clean up copy written by someone else. He is also the man who gets most of the publicity releases the city editor has decided might have some news value. Since the quality of press releases ranges from excellent to execrable, most editors want them checked for accuracy and rewritten before they are published.

The rewrite man is a fact-finder, knowing whom to call and where to look for information. When he takes a story from a leg man, he checks it where necessary, adds whatever information he needs that the man on the spot was unable to obtain, and turns the typewritten copy in to the city desk.

When the news story—that fire or parade or re-written press release—leaves the rewriteman's typewriter, it is no longer a story; it has become "copy." And here newspaper jargon sets in in earnest.

Copy is typed on "books," sandwiches of copy paper and carbon paper that produce several copies of the story, providing the city desk and the rewriteman with "dupes." Each page is a "take," and each take carries the story's "slug"—a short, indentifying word such as FIRE or PARADE or PTA. The first take also carries the last name of the rewrite man and of the reporter or reporters from whom he took his information.

(When the rewrite man is writing against a deadline, copy is fed, a take at a time, to the city desk and copy desk. This is when you will hear cries of "Boy!" "Boy!" as copy boys are called to rush the takes from the typewriter to the editor.)

Once the copy has been glanced at and noted by the city editor—or on many papers, the news editor—it is funneled to the copy desk.

The Copyreader Takes Over

The copyreader, or copy editor, is the newspaper's main line of defense against error—the spectre that haunts all newspapermen. The reporter is trained to get his facts straight, but time and events don't always cooperate with him. The rewrite man, too, checks his story for accuracy, but since he is also human and often writing against a deadline, his typewriter also has a margin for error.

The copyreader backstops both the reporter and the rewrite man. He makes certain all information is correct, that words and names are spelled right, and that grammar and diction are correct, that the newspaper's style (each paper has its own) is followed, and that the copy does not contain any dangerous or harmful statements.

He also marks the copy so that the printer will know how to set it (one column wide or two, in bold face or italic, etc.) and he writes the headlines.

It is the city editor or the news editor who decides what kind of a headline a story deserves, and it is the copyreader who writes it. Newspapers have their own, individual styles for headlines, and they're usually labeled and graded according to importance and size. A "number five head" may be just one line of 24-point type, "number four" may be two lines.

Newspaper columns are narrow, and rubber type is still a composing-room joke, so each letter that goes into a headline has to be carefully counted if the line is to fit the space. It takes a lot of skill to squeeze the juice of a story into an understandable head, and the men who do it day after day justly pride themselves on their speed and their wit.

Between copyreaders and rewritemen there is a feud of long standing, though primarily fictional, bitterness. To the writer whose precious prose is pencilled into a paragraph, copyreaders are "comma chasers" without heart or imagination. To the copyreaders, a rewriteman is a semi-literate who thinks grammar is his mother's mother, and who has only a nodding acquaintance with the English language. "Butcher!" says the writer. "Surgeon!" answers the copyreader.

It doesn't help when a copyreader puts the surprise ending of a feature story in the head. Or when he glibly borrows for his headline a clever turn of phrase which the writer has proudly and painfully produced. In print it invariably reads as though the writer borrowed from the headline.

This is probably why most non-newspaper people— and a surprising number of publicists—think the reporter writes his own headlines. He doesn't. He wouldn't dare, even if he could, which most can't.

Copyreaders usually work side by side at a U-shaped arrangement of desks or a horseshoe-shaped table, ranged around the "rim." On the inside, in the "slot," sits the chief copyreader (the "slotman," naturally) who deals out the stories as they arrive. The individual copyreaders then go to work carefully but rapidly, marking the copy with cryptic symbols that make sense to the printers for whom they're intended.

The Composing Room

Now that the account of the fire has been phoned in by the reporter, written in six takes by the rewrite man, edited and headlined on the copy desk, it is ready for the printers. On a large newspaper, it goes to the composing room by way of pneumatic tubes. On a small weekly, the printer may just stroll into the front office and pick it up.

On the big daily, the copy cutter (or composing room superintendent or foreman) receives the copy, stamps it with the time of its arrival on his desk, and distributes it to the compositors—men who operate typesetting machines such as the Linotype or Intertype.

The Linotype

The Linotype does just what its name implies: It sets one line of type at a time. Before Ottmar Mergenthaler, a German immigrant, perfected the machine in 1886, type was set by hand, as it still is for much job printing or for fine typographical work. That is, each letter is individually picked out of a case and set beside the next. Needless to say, this is a slow and laborious process, and no way to put out a daily paper.

The idea for a typesetting machine originated in 1866, not with Mergenthaler, who was a clockmaker, but with a group of shorthand reporters in Washington, D.C. They wanted a shortcut for taking notes, transcribing them in writing, and putting their reports into print. Their interest led to the development of the dictaphone, the typewriter and, through Mergenthaler, to the Lino-

53

type. (The Intertype, also widely used in newspaper plants, was produced in 1913 on the expired patents of the Linotype, with some additions.)

But, back to the news story. Thanks to Mr. Mergenthaler's invention, which made possible the incredible output of today's daily newspapers, that four-alarm fire or parade or PTA election will get into the paper, even though the story came in shortly before deadline. The copy cutter, instead of giving all six takes of the story to one man to set, gives one take each to six different typesetters—thus speeding up its completion in time to make the edition.

The compositor now has the fire story on the machine in front of him and begins tapping out the letters on the keyboard. This is somewhat more complicated than a typewriter keyboard, and the arrangement of the letters is different, but is not difficult to learn. Every time a key is tapped, a brass matrix (a letter mold) drops into an "accumulating line" which is the exact width of the printed column. When the line is filled with brass "mats," it is pressed up against a steel mold, and molten type metal is squirted into the brass letter molds. The metal quickly chills and hardens and is ejected as a metal slug with letters on top—all ready for printing.

Large newspapers may have as many as 77 typesetting machines running at the same time, and the sound of the day's news rattling down through them is one of the most cheerful noises in the newspaper business.

As the lines of type accumulate, they are racked in long, black trays or "galleys," and on a small press, long, galley-sized strips of paper are pressed against the inked type. These are "proofs," which are sent to proofreaders who check them for typographical errors such as wrong letters, transposed letters or lines, or the famous "etaoin shrdlu" which manages to sneak into print every now and then.

These "words" so familiar to newspaper readers are composed of the letters in two vertical rows down the middle of the Linotype keyboard. When a compositor hits a wrong key, he can't "x" out the error as he might on a typewriter, and he can't take the time to pick out the incorrect letters and put them back, as he can when he's setting type by hand. Instead, he must fill up an entire line which can then be thrown away. So he quickly runs his index fingers down the two rows of letters and, voila! "etaoin shrdlu."

Make Up

The six takes of the fire story (or the parade or PTA election) by now have been set in type, gathered onto one galley, and proofed. Now they go to other printers in the composing room who will put them into the "form."

The form is a large metal frame the size of a newspaper page. It lies on a "stone," (a long table) and into it the printers pack all the type, the ads and pictures that combine to make up one page. They don't just toss it in any which-way, however. The editorial make-up man has drawn a diagram called a "dummy" showing exactly where everything should go—a two-column picture in the upper right-hand corner, a story under it, a one-column picture in the middle of the story, an A & P ad on the lower left, and so forth.

Everything is packed in tight because the form has to be lifted or slid off the stone, and no one wants the middle falling out. A locked-up form is extremely heavy, since everything in it is metal—type, ads, pictures.

Picture's Progress

The photographer who was sent to cover the fire took his first pictures as quickly as possible and hurried back to the office with them. Or he may have sent back an assistant with the film holder or roll, while he stayed with the fire.

This would assure his getting further developments on film and possibly making a more dramatic picture for use in later editions. Back at the newspaper office, the film is developed, photographic prints are made—usually on 8 x 10 glossy paper—and the picture is on its way.

First the picture editor selects the print he thinks best and sends it to the caption writers who prepare the written copy that will accompany it in the paper. Writing clear, bright and witty captions against a deadline (or even at leisure) is a fine art, and good caption writers are valued members of the editorial staff.

Then the print goes to the newspaper's art department, and the caption copy goes to the copy desk. Here the copyreaders go over it like any other copy, checking it for style and accuracy, and sending it down to the composing room. Both the print and the copy carry the same slug line and size identifications so that they can be sure of getting together again in the composing room.

The man in the art department prepares the photographic print for the photoengraver by sharpening the highlights, toning down the background or extraneous matter, and generally bringing the tones of light and dark into relationships that produce a sharp, clear picture in print.

Photoengraving

In the engraving department, the print is fastened to a copy board, and the photoengraver takes a picture of it through a halftone screen which breaks up the lights and darks into little dots. The resulting negative is assembled (along with other negatives) on a sheet of heavy plate glass which is then laid face down on a sheet of zinc coated with a solution sensitive to light.

Both the zinc plate and glass plate are held in position and placed in a photoprinting machine and exposed to bright light. A photo print is now being made on metal instead of on paper. The metal sheet is processed through several acid baths that remove the metal that wasn't exposed to light and leave those dots that were.

It is the dots that print. In a newspaper picture, what looks black to the naked eye is really a massing of dots, while what looks white is really a wider spacing of dots.

The picture is now a piece of metal cut to the exact size it will appear in the paper, and it is sent from the engraving department to the composing room to be assembled, along with the ads and the type, in the form. The words and the pictures are backward. When paper is pressed against their inked surfaces, they will be reversed and readable.

Going to Press

If this were a small newspaper plant with limited circulation, the form would probably go from the stone directly to the flatbed, cylinder press, and the papers would be printed directly off the type, one sheet at a time.

However, the thousands of impressions required by large newspapers would soon pound the type metal into mush, to say nothing of taking days to print. Modern newspapers presses are rotary presses. Long ribbons of newsprint are fed between clyinders much the same as mother fed the wet sheets into the wringer of the old-fashioned washing machine.

One cylinder presses the ribbon of paper against another on which is locked the newspaper page, converted from a flat, jigsaw puzzle of type metal and zinc plates into a solid, curved sheet of metal.

The means by which a flat metal page becomes a curved metal page is called stereotyping.

When the form containing the finished page moves into the stereo room, a sheet of special paper is pressed hard down upon it, producing a paper mold of the page. This sheet is bent into semi-cylindrical shape corresponding to the curve of the press cylinder and placed in a casting machine where molten metal is poured against it.

What comes out is a curved metal plate bearing the reproduction of the page form. This is clamped onto the press cylinders, and the news of the day begins to roll.

The rotary press in action is a wondrous and thunderous thing to watch. Weaving and interweaving, endless ribbons of newsprint thread their way through the maze of drums and wheels and webbing. The press room is a roaring canyon, and the air is rich with the smell of printer's ink and oil and the dry scent of newsprint. At the far end of the press, the newspaper emerges, cut and folded and assembled, with all its pages marvelously in order.

Up to the mailing room and onto the trucks the papers go. The ink is still wet, and the newsprint warm when they are tossed on to street corners at newsstands throughout the city.

4

WORKING WITH
THE CITY DESK

To THE publicity man or woman, probably the most important area of a newspaper is the city desk. No matter how many columnists may call you by your first name, or how many departmental editors you can reach on the telephone, you are not really in business until you know the city desk, understand its functions, and know how to work with everyone in the city room from the city editor to the reporter on the beat.

The city desk generally is considered the heartbeat of the newspaper. It is here, under the supervision and guidance of the City Editor, that the local news of the day is gathered, digested and written.

And it is here that every publicity man worth his expense account will find himself working hard and often before he retires to write the Great American Novel. For this is where you direct your press releases when you feel you have a story of general news interest. And this is where you turn when you want to request the attendance of a reporter at an important meeting, major luncheon, civic celebration or other similar special event.

In fact (although the feeders of columns and the haunters of woman's departments will howl at the thought) , city-side handling of a publicity story or event is pretty high up on the publicity man's table of values. For when the city side uses your story in the general news columns of the paper, or assigns reporters to cover your special event, you have brought off a coup.

Your story, your event, are no longer just publicity . . . they're news.

Of course, everything an organization may do, produce, or announce may not necessarily be "city side" news. Your releases, in this case, might more logically be directed to a specialized section of the paper, such as business, society, fashion, entertainment, and others.

If you're not sure whether your event, story, or request legitimately should go to the city desk, ask yourself the following questions about it:

1. Is the story truly news of general interest? That is, will anyone outside the select group you represent really care to read about it?

2. Is it fresh and timely, about-to-happen, not just an old story with a new slant?

3. Is your information correct and complete—do you have all the facts?

If you have answered "yes" to each of these, go ahead and make your contact.

Deadlines

At this point, of course, it is assumed that you are thoroughly familiar with the deadline schedules of all the newspapers in town, so you don't lose your coverage through bad timing.

You can't hope to do a good publicity job for any organization without knowing the deadlines of the newspapers you are dealing with. This applies not only to the city desk, but to every other section or department of the newspaper as well.

The deadline determines when your release should be on the editor's desk; at what hour your photo assignment tip (see Chapter 6) should land on the picture desk; and how late you can hope to get a late-breaking story or picture into a particular edition.

Originally a deadline was a line drawn around a prison to indicate the point beyond which a prisoner could not go without being shot. It's not much different in the newspaper business today. The deadline indicates the last possible moment at which a story can still get into an edition. If you go beyond that deadline, your release is dead.

Deadlines are even more important when you are "creating" rather than just reporting the news, as, for example, when you stage an outdoor fashion show in the courthouse square. You will have to time your announcements, stunts or events in such a way that every paper can meet its particular deadline and still not be scooped by another.

If your timing has favored the morning papers, for instance, you can't very well blame the afternoons if they do not run what is, by then, an old story.

Newspaper deadlines are no secret. All you have to do is phone the papers, tell them what you want to know, and they'll be happy to give you the information. Good professional handling on your part in effect adds a reporter to the news staff—and makes life easier for everyone on the city desk.

The City Editor

Once your publicity release lands on the city desk, it will be the city editor who decides whether your story belongs in the paper in the first place, and how much space it's worth, in the second.

Decisions like this, and hundreds that are far more complex, make the city editor's job one of the toughest in the newspaper business. And no matter what the movies or television try to tell you, the real McCoy is not a fast-talking, hard drinking, hard-cursing tyrant. More than likely he is a hard-working, down-to-earth professional who knows that to get out a good newspaper he's got to be a juggler, diplomat, psychologist, efficiency expert and crystal ball reader.

The city editor is boss in the city room where working under him are copy boys and various assistants, photographers, miscellaneous editors, and, of course, the reporting staff. These are:

Beat men, who cover regular news runs such as police, courts and labor,

Leg men, who go out on stories on assignment, phoning in the facts and information,

Rewrite men, who stay in the office to write stories coming in from the leg men and other sources.

Not only does the city editor have the responsibility for coordinating the wildly various efforts of all these people, but he also has the less-than-fascinating chore of wading through hundreds of unsolicited press releases and taking dozens of unsolicited phone calls from amateur and professional publicity people each day. Many of those releases and phone calls, we might add, are essential in helping him round out the day's news.

For today's city editor is a man with his finger on the city's pulse. He knows his town inside out. He knows what's happening today, what happened yesterday, and what's going to happen tomorrow. He knows almost everything that's been printed—and quite a few things that can't be printed.

The good will of this man is essential to any organization or individual seeking publicity in the general news columns of the daily paper.

Getting Along With the City Editor

Although you may never have met the city editor of your local paper, and may never even have made one of those unsolicited telephone calls, chances are that he has formed some image of you on the basis of the publicity techniques you employ.

Every editor, of course, has his own, personal peeves, things you might do that could put you on his hate list. These you will have to discover for yourself, through discreet questions, tactful handling, trial and error. But there are some publicity practices that are guaranteed to make you *persona non grata* with almost any city editor in the land, and these we can help you avoid.

We list them without any attempt to assess their IQ (irritation quotient) :

Shoddy releases, long-winded telephone calls, persistent visits, and outside pressure.

Shoddy releases are those which are badly written, bursting with adjectives, inaccurate, overlong, and entirely devoid of news interest. Just give him the facts, and the city editor will take it from there.

Long-winded and frequent telephone calls have no place in the city room. Keep them short and to the point, and make them only when time is a factor or when the information cannot be presented better in writing.

Persistent personal visits to the city room cut into an editor's busy schedule. Keep these to the barest minimum, and if you must make a personal call, get in and get out fast.

The greatest sin of all, of course, is the application of outside pressure, the kind, for instance, that might be brought to bear by "good advertisers."

Nothing can make an enemy of a city editor more quickly than the intrusion of some other department—circulation, advertising, business office—into the sacred precincts of "editorial." You might get away with it once, but after that you may just as well turn in your typewriter. You won't be getting cooperation from that city desk again!

William F. McIlwain, Jr., City Editor of *Newsday*, one of America's leading newspapers, was explicit in his analysis of the relations between publicity people and the newspaper.

"It's easy for publicity people to get along with newspapermen if they approach their job right," he said.

"When they've got good, legitimate stories, they shouldn't press too hard. They should make available the necessary factual material—then leave the rest to the newspaper.

"In other words, they shouldn't try to look over the editor's shoulder, coming up with all sorts of angles and directing the story to its conclusion. Any good newspaper knows what it wants, and how it wants the story told—so the publicity people should put forth the facts, then step back out of it."

You as a publicity man or woman can win the confidence and cooperation of the city editor by obeying one simple rule: Keep him informed.

This precept is so simple and so basic that it is often overlooked. One of the nation's most famous city editors, Frank S. Adams, of *The New York Times* is emphatic on this point: "All news releases should be sent to the city desk of a newspaper," he says, "in addition to any reporters who may normally handle this type of news.

"You would be amazed to know how often public relations men send out releases to reporters whom they mistakenly assume would be likely to handle a given story, and do not send a duplicate copy to the city desk.

"If the reporter is absent, off sick, or out of town, the release languishes in his mailbox and the story is not printed. This happened recently in the case of a story with Page One importance from one of the largest organizations in the health field. The release was sent to two reporters, one of whom was sick and the other out of town, with the result that we knew nothing about it until we saw it in a competing newspaper. This does not develop good will with an organization that follows such a practice."

Working With the Reporter

As Mr. Adams indicated, it's a mistake to send a news release to a reporter on the assumption that he will then handle the story. A reporter will almost never cover your event—or even follow up your publicity release—without having been assigned to do so by the city editor or his assistant.

As a matter of fact, unless you're the public relations spokesman for a decision-making organization, the press representative for a "hard-to-get ticket" show, or press agent for a "hot" personality or political figure, you will more often be in the position of trying to break your material "cold."

However, at one time or another during your life as a publicity man, you're going to get a phone call from a newspaper. Usually such calls are most welcome, but there are times when they produce something less than rapture in the heart of the publicity man with a problem.

This is because there are really only two important reasons why a reporter should be calling you:

1. Either you have sent out a release that is incomplete and the paper needs more information, or,

2. From a number of sources—none of them necessarily you—the newspaper "smells" a story in your organization.

In either case, you must be prepared to take care of the inquiring reporter in every possible way.

Frequently, if it's merely a matter of filling in information, you can supply the missing details over the phone.

However, if the information required is lengthy or complex, or if the reporter wants to talk to some of your top people, you will have to set an appointment date.

If the reporter is checking out a story that might prove embarrassing to your organization, you will have to be particularly tactful. In such a situation you can destroy at one stroke your present, and future, relationship with the newspaper.

The best practice is to open up and cooperate to the best of your ability—or, at least, to the extent that policy will allow. This is the kind of practice that will earn you the respect of the press, and, we may add, assure your organization of a fair hearing at all times.

If, however, you or your management have decided upon a policy of silence, at least give the reporter a "no comment" that he can use. But don't duck his calls.

It is a dismaying fact that too often in such a situation, public relations people suddenly become scarcer than taxis in a thunderstorm, although these are the same people who just yesterday were badgering the papers for publicity and who probably will be badgering them again tomorrow.

The best policy to follow when a reporter queries you on a story that you don't want told is:

Tell it. Tell it fully and honestly, giving all sides.

Not only is this the honorable and fair approach, it's also tactically the best. For if a reporter is worth his weekly paycheck, he'll get the story anyway, from other sources, despite your lack of cooperation.

The important difference will be that you'll have lost the opportunity to tell your side of it.

On the other hand, when a solid, legitimate news story develops, don't wait for some sharp reporter to stumble on it or ferret it out. *You* tell it—and tell it not just to one favored reporter or newspaper, but to every one in town. You'll find that the next time you are trying to "sell" a marginal story—one that's hardly earthshaking in its import—you will probably get a more favorable hearing.

If the reporter who calls is up against a deadline, you'll have to be prepared to move heaven, earth and the board of directors to accommodate him. But if no deadline is involved, and the appointment time he wants is impossible for you or your staff, don't hesitate to tell him so. Reporters are people, too, and only a few are prima donnas.

In any case, don't act hastily. Try to give yourself enough time to round up the requested information and/or top brass.

To Eat or Not to Eat

There is one more point to be made concerning reporters: It's not necessary to feed them.

It's surprising how many publicity beginners (and old timers, too) still believe that a reporter is some half-starved waif who is thrilled silly at the prospect of getting a free meal every time he gets an assignment. It just ain't necessarily so. Reporters today make a pretty fair salary and are generally a well-fed lot. They're much more likely to be trying to get rid of a few pounds than looking for chances to put them on.

More important, they're busy. Even as you and I, they're either too rushed for a long, sit-down lunch or they prefer to break bread with good friends where lunch will be pleasure—not business.

One reporter on a large metropolitan daily puts it this way:

"I don't like to work on my lunch hour, no matter how fancy the restaurant. Ocassionally it's a good way to get acquainted with the publicity man and to fill him in on what type of news you cover, and so forth. But I don't like to interview his client in a noisy, crowded restaurant.

"For one thing, I can't eat and take notes at the same time. The food gets cold, and the notes get spotted with salad dressing. Anyway, I would much prefer to interview the client in his office where I can ask questions without being interrupted by the waiter."

So, save the luncheon invitation for a reporter you

have come to know, one who might conceivably consider lunch with you in the line of pleasure, as well as business.

Of course, there will be some reporters who consider the lunch-interview a highly productive way of gathering information for a story. In this case, by all means, go to lunch.

The simplest way to solve the problem is merely to ask. If the invitation is accepted, then choose a restaurant conducive to quiet conversation. If the answer is "no lunch," then arrange to get together at a time convenient to everyone.

Getting the Breaks

The reporter has called, you've cooperated, and now he has all the information he needs to write your story fairly and fully. That doesn't mean that the story will run.

At this point you can only assume that if the city editor has assigned someone to get the story, you might have a 50-50 chance of seeing it in print. Whether you ever do will depend heavily upon the nature and news value of your story.

And even if it's solid, straight news and the city editor and reporter both believe fervently that it should appear in the paper— don't count on it. Between the time your story is set in type and the time the edition goes to press, anything from a hurricane to a society suicide can knock it right out of the paper. Many a costly and time-consuming special event of good local interest never saw the light of print or was boiled down to a few inches of type because of last minute big news.

These sudden and dramatic news developments can be as frustrating to the editor as to the publicity man.

Joseph Herzberg, former Night City Editor of *The New York Herald Tribune*, underscored this problem in a speech explaining the work of the *Tribune's* city room:

"As the day progresses, the picture of the paper begins to take shape. You begin to know which are the important stories you're going to have tomorrow. You know which are the minor ones. You know some can be dropped out. And you know also, that at any given time, something may happen that is considerably more important than any single thing you have in the paper . . .

"Stories like that don't come too frequently, but things happen with tremendous speed . . . and within the hour . . . the whole point of view for the paper (may be) changed."

You can hardly be expected to time your publicity or special event not to compete with news that hasn't happened yet, but you can avoid conflicts with the many news-making events which are advertised well in advance.

Among the baker's dozen of sources listing forthcoming news-making community events are the Department of Commerce, the local convention bureau or Chamber of Commerce, your local newspaper's information department, and the police department, which issues permits for street fairs and other such events.

A Word About the Managing Editor

The presence of the Managing Editor is very much felt on the city desk although his responsibilities are by no means confined to its activities alone. More than a newsman, the managing editor is an executive who deals in the over-all affairs of management as well as the daily job of getting out the newspaper. He helps to determine the subject and slant of the day's editorials, and he has an important voice in the final make-up of the paper. The city editor is responsible to him, as are all the other department editors.

Caution: Confine your publicity activities to the newspaper's department heads. Not only will the managing editor generally be of no assistance to you in the processing of publicity, but going to him over the heads of his editors can seriously impair your relations with them.

A Word About Honesty

During the researching of this book, the subject of honesty in publicity and public relations has recurred repeatedly. In speeches and articles, editors, reporters and public relations authorities have stressed the need for an honest presentation of news on the part of the publicity man.

It would seem axiomatic that dishonesty in publicity is as unproductive in the long run as dishonesty in any other form of business or personal endeavor. However, since the newspaper industry is founded upon the accurate presentation of unvarnished facts, honesty in dealing with newspapermen is not only the best policy, it's downright essential to survival.

Today, publicity and public relations are recognized as important allies of journalism. Few editors or reporters will ignore the existence of a publicity person the first time around when they're gathering information about an organization or business enterprise. If the publicity man does his job well—that is, if he services the reporter fully and honestly—the relationship can only prosper, ultimately erasing the shadow of doubt and distrust.

At a recent public relations workshop, Fene Hess, Night City Editor of *The Philadelphia Inquirer,* summed up matters this way:

"Don't trick us. Be frank with us and we'll cooperate. You have to eat, we have to eat, and we both have to inform."

5

PREPARING
THE PRESS RELEASE

SUCCESSFUL PUBLICITY and the press release are very much like love and marriage—you seldom can have one without the other.

Like the carpenter's hammer or the bricklayer's trowel, the press release is an important tool in the publicity man's kit. You cannot build an effective publicity program without it. Fortunately for us all, carpenters and bricklayers employ their tools with much more care and skill than most publicity people apply to the press release.

Generally speaking, the press release (or news release, publicity release or handout) can be defined as a communique from the publicity man to the newspaperman, bringing to his attention a timely piece of information about some company, organization or other special interest group.

So far as the newspaper is concerned, the press release is "the" accepted method of communication between newspaperman and publicity man, and fully 75 per cent of all contacts between the two groups are made in this way. Where most phone calls will get a fast brush-off, and personal visits a cold, lonely wait, the press release will receive immediate attention.

Whether it can hold that attention depends entirely upon the publicity man who sent the release. It is unfortunately true that most press releases today are badly conceived, based on poor judgment, badly written and presented, and, as often as not, sent to the wrong editor!

As a consequence, the majority of all press releases wind up in the "circular file," lining wastebaskets in newspaper offices from coast to coast.

Let's face it, it costs money to operate a newspaper (or magazine), and editors can't afford to staff their papers with sufficient personnel to select, evaluate and rewrite all the stuff that pours in daily from outside sources. It's up to the publicity man to turn out the kind of releases that will win acceptance.

For Immediate Discard

A study conducted by the *Lock Haven (Penna.) Express*, a small daily, in cooperation with the state's Society of Newspaper Editors, documented some important reasons why so many releases are missing their mark, failing so miserably to achieve their objectives.

For two weeks all releases received—and rejected—by *The Express* were kept and filed instead of crumpled up and thrown away. In all, 383 releases from 182 sources were turned down. Although the majority came from commercial sources, the rejects included a number from public service agencies as well. At the end of two weeks, an analysis of the discards was made. Following are the major reasons why these releases would have ended in the wastebasket:

1. No local angle
2. Lack of timeliness
3. Poor news writing

4. Too long
5. Too commercial
6. Sneaking company names into seemingly inconspicuous places
7. Gearing releases more to influence editors than actually to provide material for the news columns

Charles Seller, reporting on the study for *Editor and Publisher*, the newspaper industry's trade journal, concluded that publicists are "more concerned with quantity than quality—or ignorant of how to write a news story and what a handout must contain to *be* a news story."

The results of this survey are by no means isolated or unique to one particular section of Pennsylvania. The University of Wisconsin announced similar findings after questioning sixty newspaper editors across the country on the same subject.

Writing the Release

Assuming that you will henceforth avoid the Seven Deadly Sins listed above, here is what you can do to assure consideration of your release when it reaches the editor's desk.

First, make sure you really have something to tell.

Then tell it in clear and simple language.

Despite the King of Heart's advice to Alice, the best way to tell a story to a newspaper is NOT "to begin at the beginning and go until you come to the end, then stop." A release should embody only the facts essential to the news of the story. The need for additional information to "round-out" the story should be determined by the editor.

A well-constructed news release should answer these six important questions:

1. What is happening?
2. Who is involved in it?
3. When is it taking place?
4. Where is it taking place?
5. How is it being done?
6. Why?

Adhering to this formula does not necessarily mean your release has to sound like an excerpt from an encyclopedia. You can still tell your story with interest and color without wandering from the essentials. Lewis Jordan, News Editor of *The New York Times,* puts it this way in the introduction to his pamphlet, "News, How It Is Written and Edited:"

"Writing a story for a newspaper should be like writing a letter to a friend. A good letter writer will send to his friend a full and clear account of what has happened since the last letter. That is what the friend wants. The writer will tell about the big and important things, but will not leave out the little things. They also are important."

Mr. Jordan, of course, is talking primarily to the writer on the newspaper. A publicity man would add one more thought:

"Write your letter as though your friend is on the move and has little time for reading."

A good press release should incorporate all salient facts in the very first paragraph, in clear and simple language. We cannot stress this fact enough, since the average newspaper editor, reporter or columnist usually judges the story on the basis of the first paragraph.

Marie Torre, former TV columnist for *The New York Herald Tribune,* says:

"I seldom read beyond the first paragraph, depending

on what it is, of course. Most of the time I can tell by the first paragraph what the entire thing is about, and I discard it."

Once you've compressed the gist of the story in the first paragraph, the balance of your release can add other relevant details.

For example: When announcing the promotion of a company executive, the first paragraph should state, simply:

Who	*"Mr. John P. Jones* has been
What	*appointed Vice President* in charge of
Where	sales for the *XYZ Division* of the
	ABC Company, Inc.,"

The second paragraph would then enlarge upon this fact:

	"Mr. Jones, formerly assistant to the
	Vice President, has been with the
Why	ABC Company ten years. *He replaces*
	William B. Smith who is retiring."

The balance of the release should briefly explain the duties of the new job and give in capsule the functions of the company. The release might also include a brief statement from the top officer of the company explaining the move, and might end with a brief biography of Mr. Jones— his education, past positions, place of residence.

Just how much detail you should include or logically expect to see in print is a matter of perspective. If the company is a small one, such an announcement might not get a single line in a large city daily. It might rate a paragraph in the "area page" of a small city daily. And in Mr. Jones's hometown weekly, it probably would be given a half column and a photograph to boot!

Other announcements may not lend themselves to so

simple a presentation as Mr. Jones's promotion did, but the principles involved in writing the release are identical. A release directed to the Woman's Page of a local newspaper might look like this:

What	"The fourth annual Spring flower show
Who	sponsored by the Smalltown Conservation
When	Club Auxiliary will be held May 19 and 20
Where	in the Masonic Temple on Center St.
Why	Proceeds of the show will be used to finance the establishment of a wild bird refuge on the northern shore of Lake George. Mrs. A. B. Cecil, president of the auxiliary, said chairman appointments will be made at the full membership meeting next week."

Before they attempt to write the release, beginners in the field of publicity would do well to study the style and presentation of news stories in the sections of the papers they want to reach. This does not mean copying their style, but it does mean being aware of the fact that they do have a style.

Each newspaper prides itself on its own particular style, and most of them even publish style books for distribution to staff members so that everything written for publication will be permeated with it. A story appearing in *The New York Times,* for instance, certainly would sound a great deal different from the same story in *The New York Daily News.* Yet each story would embody the same facts. The difference would lie in the style of presentation.

Your release may never appear in print in the form in which it was originally sent (releases seldom do), but if your writing shows some awareness of the newspaper's style and needs, your chances of being read and accepted are vastly improved.

What Goes Into the Release

Nothing is so frustrating to a reporter or editor as to be confronted with an incomplete, badly-turned-out press release. Since the release is the primary point of contact between publicity man and newspaperman, it can also, if badly handled, become a primary source of irritation. Surprisingly enough, it is not only the beginners who err in this area, but the publicity veterans as well.

Every press release should include the following information:

1. Name of organization
2. Address of organization
3. Phone number of organization
4. Name and office phone number and extension of person responsible for the release
5. Home or night phone number of person responsible for the release
6. Date release is sent out*
7. Requested release date**

There is no excuse for sending out a release that lacks this essential information.

Christina Kirk, reporter on *The New York Herald Tribune,* is emphatic on this point:

* *Note:* This information is usually typed directly before first word of first paragraph. (See sample release)
**Note:* This should appear flush with the right-hand margin and should look like this: "FOR RELEASE ON THURSDAY, JUNE 5."

"My biggest complaint about press releases," says Miss Kirk, "is that many of them do not contain the most basic information needed by the reporter. For example, I get releases on letterheads that say only: 'Blank Company, For Immediate Release.'

"That's all. No date, no address, no telephone number, no name. How is the reporter supposed to know how long this release has been kicking around the office? If he has a question, how does he know whom to call?

"Sometimes the release will give a clue: a phone number, but not the extension. So you get the company switchboard and you say, 'May I have your public relations department?' And the operator says, 'Is it about an ad? Do you want to buy something? Who do you want to talk to?' (You have no way of knowing.) Finally she says, 'I'll give you the personnel department.' And then you go through the whole routine again."

Miss Kirk's experience may seem far-fetched to the reader who has been meticulous in this vital area of press relations, but among members of the working press, hers is just one more voice in a chorus that can be heard in newspaper offices throughout the country.

What It Should Look Like

All press releases look alike, regardless of the kind of story they tell or the kind of organization sending them.

- A release must always be typed, never handwritten.
- It should appear double-spaced on a standard 8½ x 11 sheet of paper, on one side of the sheet only.

news COMPANY NAME, ADDRESS AND PHONE NUMBER

FOR IMMEDIATE RELEASE

April 23, 1965

CONTACT:

YOUR NAME
Phone Ext:
Home Phone:

SAMPLE PRESS RELEASE

- Margins should allow plenty of editing room—about an inch-and-a-half (or 15 typewriter spaces) on each side.
- Never send out carbons. They smudge and they're hard to read and they imply a lack of respect for the ultimate reader. If the release is going to a select group of publications—seven or fewer—type each copy individually. If it is being sent out in large numbers, have it mimeographed.
- Few releases need to be longer than two pages.

Experience has proved that almost any story, properly written, with all adjectives and flowery phrases boiled out, can be told in two pages. More than this presents a discouraging prospect to the newspaperman who usually looks upon a press release as an intrusion on his valuable time.

You will be tempted to write much more in the hope that your story will receive proportionately more space in print. Don't do it. If your story commands or deserves more space, the editor will make that decision.

The Release Date

A requested release date assures your story of coverage by all newspapers, and at the same time it eliminates the possibility that one paper will publish your story before the others do. This occassionally happens, and when it does, the reaction among the newspapers which were "scooped" is usually one of resentment toward the organization.

A specified release date also allows an editor time to assign a reporter to cover the story and still be sure of breaking it at the same time it appears in the other papers.

One way to improve your chances with both morning and afternoon papers is to send out especially-tailored variations of the same story—one slanted to the needs of the morning papers and the other to the needs of the afternoon publications. This is particularly important if your release date must be strictly observed.

(As noted in Chapter 4, "Working With the City Desk," a story that appears in a morning paper is old news to that day's afternoon papers.)

When you do send out two versions of the same release, one should be labeled: FOR MORNING PAPERS, and the other, FOR AFTERNOON PAPERS.

When your story is urgent and timely, the release date reads: FOR IMMEDIATE RELEASE.

This eliminates all flexibility and tells the editor in so many words that it is now or never. A release sent to the city desk bearing such an immediate release date is usually discarded if it's not used after the first day or two. However, many editors of special sections have been known to hold a release for as long as a week or two before using it.

Headlines

The most important point to remember about writing headlines on news releases is: DON'T.

Editors have been known to react violently and negatively to headlines on press releases. Such a practice presumes to tell the editor what the news value of the story is and exactly how it should be headed.

Not only is this presumptuous, it's also a waste of time. Newspaper headlines are graded in size and are constructed according to the size and kind of type used. Moreover, editors and reporters don't write headlines. If they know what's good for them, they won't even *suggest* headlines. Newspapers have their own headline writers, men who are skilled at compressing the gist of a story into a painfully limited space. They won't appreciate having you or anyone else trespassing in their domain.

Worst of all, a headline on your press release implies that you don't really think the editor is going to read it anyway, so you try to catch his attention with a tricky or dramatic heading.

Many organizations get around the ticklish headline problem by typing a brief summary of the story at the upper left hand side of the release. This gives the editor the essence of the story at a glance without (it is hoped) ruffling his feathers. However, most newspaper editors say the best policy is simply to tell the story and leave the headline and the summary to the newspaper professionals.

Often the publicity person's joy upon finding his story in the paper is dimmed by the fact that the headline is misleading, inadvertently changing the meaning of the story.

A case in point was a delightful story about the unexpected birth of a set of kangaroos in a department store's Christmas "zoo." The headline read:

"PROBLEMS AT GIMBELS MULTIPLY"

This, of course, gave the entire story a negative connotation, but slips like this are an occupational hazard, and there isn't much you can do about it except to learn to accept it philosophically—and hope that your boss, or client, or organization will be as understanding of the vicissitudes of the newspaper business.

Of course, if the headline or any part of the story carries an outright error, there is nothing wrong with your calling the paper to make a correction for later editions.

Getting the Release There

Releases may be sent to the newspapers either by messenger or through the mails. When the importance and timeliness of a story warrants, by all means send it by messenger. If time is not of the essence, your release will be perfectly safe in the mails. Releases are not discarded just because they come by mail, and a poor release, whether it's delivered by hand or on a velvet cushion, might just as well never have left home in the first place.

Timing

The proper timing of your release can spell the difference between success or failure of your publicity effort. For best results in this important area, we suggest the following schedule:

a. If your release date is TUESDAY, OCTOBER 7 —MORNING PAPERS—the release should be on the editor's desk no later than Monday, 10 a.m., October 6th.

b. If your date is TUESDAY, OCTOBER 7— AFTERNOON PAPERS—the release should be on the editor's desk about 4 p.m., Monday, October 6th.

c. If your date is TUESDAY, OCTOBER 7, for both afternoon and morning papers, it is advisable to send out the releases separately, each following the schedule above.

Some publicity people will send out their story two, three or more days in advance of the release date with these special instructions for the editor: "HOLD FOR RELEASE ON TUESDAY, OCTOBER 7." If the story is strong enough, the editor might file the release in his "futures" file and use it on the requested date of release; however, the "hold for the future" story is fraught with dangers which could cause you to miss publication altogether. For one thing, the release could be lost—this has happened before. For another, one newspaper might inadvertently print it earlier than requested, scooping the other papers.

The timing of special event releases varies from that of the standard release. This subject is discussed in Chapter 7, "Accommodating the Press." Other timing details are covered in Chapter 4, "Working With the City Desk."

A final word: Regardless of what editor or department your release is directed to, be sure that at least one copy goes to the desk of the city editor as well, and mark both releases with a notation to that effect. City editors are quite insistent on this point. Often a story which might lose out as business news could make ideal copy for the general news pages of the paper.

Follow-Up

Except for major events or stories, *do not follow up your press release with a phone call.* The query, "Did you get my release? Are you going to use it?" can serve only to antagonize rather than help. If, on the other hand, you plan a cornerstone-laying ceremony, and the press is invited, a follow-up can be a useful service to the newspaper. More on this in Chapter 7, "Accommodating the Press."

6

WORKING WITH
PICTURES AND THE PHOTO DESK

As AN IMPORTANT tool of the publicity man, the photograph ranks second only to the press release. Like the release, the picture has a story to tell. The printed word tells it in depth; the photograph tells it in an instant. The printed story catches the reader's eye; the photograph compels it.

Just as there are some stories that only the printed word can tell with dimension and thoroughness, there are others that can be more dramatically told in pictures. The arrival of a movie star at Idlewild airport, for example, can be reported in fewer than five printed lines. But a picture of that star leaving the plane can command a quarter of a page in the newspaper, and, if the star is Marilyn Monroe, even the front page of some papers.

While most of your press releases will be sent to the city editor, most of your publicity pictures will be sent to the Picture Editor. (On smaller newspapers, one man may hold both jobs. A phone call to the paper will set you straight on this point.) The only exceptions to this general rule occur when you are dealing with the fashion editor, automotive editor, church editor, and other such specialized department heads.

87

Most of the time, however, it is the picture editor whom you must learn to satisfy if you expect to see your pictures in print.

The Picture Editor

He is the man who decides which pictures will appear in each day's paper and which will be tossed onto the discard pile.* In making these decisions, he draws upon a wide variety of highly developed skills, among them solid news judgment, a knowledge of photography and photo-engraving, a better-than-nodding acquaintance with design, composition and style. A good picture editor, like a good reporter or good photographer, also has a sixth sense for that unusual and compelling element of human interest that captures the public imagination—and sells newspapers.

This is the man to whom you will be sending most of your publicity pictures. They will have to measure up to his professional standards, as well as meet some of the keenest competition in the publicity field.

Over the picture desk daily pours the output of the newspaper's own photographers as well as hundreds of pictures from accredited wire and news services and from feature syndicates. These sources alone present an enormous problem of selection and can easily fill the newspaper each day without any help from publicity people.

Nevertheless, a good publicity picture still stands a chance because picture editors are always looking for the best pictures they can find, regardless of the source. They will look at every picture that comes across the desk.

*Note: On most newspapers, the picture editor is also in charge of the photo staff, although a few large papers give this responsibility to a photo assignment editor.

Unfortunately, what comes across the desk from publicity sources is pretty bad. Although picture editors do not have to wade through millions of empty words as do their confreres on the city desk, their intelligence and good taste are nonetheless continually insulted and assaulted by the incredibly bad pictures publicity people ask them to consider.

Fully 85 to 95 per cent of all such pictures wind up in the discard. Picture editors in newspaper offices across the country are of one voice when it comes to placing the blame for this apalling waste. They point to three major flaws that inevitably appear in nearly every publicity picture:

1. Rank commercialism
2. Poor technical quality
3. Lack of imagination and creativity

Just one of these would be enough to doom a photograph, but many publicity pictures contain all three. In this area, professional publicists make the same mistakes (and make them as often) as amateurs and volunteers. The only difference is, the professionals get paid for it.

Rank Commercialism

Over-commercialism is the loudest complaint against publicity pictures. Many a newsworthy and technically excellent picture which would otherwise have made the grade has been disqualified by a scarcely-disguised "plug."

"The publicity man pushes too hard," says J. Howard Knapp, Picture Editor for *The New York Daily News,* the nation's leading picture newspaper. On an average day, Mr. Knapp looks at from 400 to 500 pictures, of which only about ninety will make the paper. Of all the rejects, the highest mortality rate occurs among publicity pictures.

"Most publicity people make no attempt to make their pictures interesting generally," says Mr. Knapp. "We don't object to a plug—they have something to sell and we want pictures. If it's a good picture, and the plug is not too blatant or too obvious, we don't mind.

"But a lot of the stuff we get is pure, out-and-out advertising matter—and we have a good advertising rate here!"

Tom Cleere, Picture Editor of *The New York Journal-American*, shares this view:

"We judge publicity pictures purely on news value and personality," he says. "Basic publicity very seldom gets into the paper. If the photo will be of benefit to the reader, we will use it. If it features a personality, it must be someone who is in the news or is otherwise newsworthy. But if it's a flagrant example of publicity, it hits the basket."

And Manny Elkins, Picture Editor of *The New York Daily Mirror*, sums up the commercialism complaint this way: "If the picture has no news value of any kind, we scrap it. An ordinary publicity picture means nothing to us."

Despite the editors' outcry against the plug, the pitch and the commercial, publicity men and women continue to ignore this fact of journalistic life. These same people are probably writing press releases for the wastebasket— and for the same reason. All in all, the result is a shameful waste of time and money.

Poor Quality

However, where a rejected press release may represent

only the writer's time, a sheet of inexpensive bond paper run off on a mimeograph, and a four-cent stamp on a business envelope, a rejected photograph is a really costly item. It represents not only the photographer's time but also that of his subjects, plus the cost of supplies and processing, and film and photo-enlarging paper are not cheap. Moreover, it takes more than one stamp as well as a special envelope to carry a picture through the mails.

In view of this investment of time and money, poor technical quality in a publicity photo is inexcusable. Yet, as Harvey Weber, Picture Editor of *Newsday* (Long Island) points out:

"The quality of the photography in this area is almost universally and absolutely atrocious. We've often remarked here at *Newsday* that if people are getting paid for this kind of stuff, it's a crime."

Publicity people, he says, apparently think that if the picture includes a beauty queen or some other kind of pretty girl, it will automatically sell itself.

"The pictures are badly lit, badly posed and badly cropped," he says. "Therefore, very little of this stuff is printed."

Howard Knapp of *The Daily News* also rates this reason high on the list of reasons why so many publicity pictures are rejected.

"Most pictures that come in from publicity people are just not good pictures technically," he says.

"For good newspaper reproduction, a half-tone needs gradation in the blacks and greys. Most pictures we get are flat, with no grading of tones, no detail in the blacks, and with whites that are burned out. We often get a picture that's a good idea but is so badly executed we can't use it."

Lack of Creativity

Lack of imagination and originality is the third *bête noir* of the picture editor plowing through the day's batch of unsolicited photographs.

Ed Stein, Night Managing Editor of *The New York Journal-American* and a former picture editor, says he is frankly appalled by the triteness and the stereotyped subjects and treatments that mark most publicity pictures.

"I realize these things have got to be keyed to some extent to satisfy the client," says Mr. Stein, "but they will never see the light of day unless they're going to satisfy an editor."

Larry VanGelder, Associate Editor of *The New York Daily Mirror* concurs:

"The volume of pictures that come in per day with four people standing behind a desk is immeasurable, and one can get awfully tired looking at them. One can dismiss them quickly unless they involve extraordinary people. More imagination is needed."

There are, of course, some subjects that just cannot be photographed any other way—and the newspaper's own staff photographers take plenty. All the more reason, one picture editor commented, that a publicity picture of that kind won't stand a chance.

As *The Journal-American's* Ed Stein pointed out:

"When you realize that white space in most newspapers is at a premium today and that these pictures are competing with the regular wire services plus the paper's own staff, I would say that a fantastically small percentage has a fighting chance at all. And they have to be outstanding or they won't be used."

Snap Judgment

In view of the picture editor's jaundiced outlook, it might be appropriate to ask whether the publicity picture is really worth the time, trouble and expense it requires. This is a question on which public relations people, educators and newspaper publishers themselves, disagree.

In fact, you can now reverse the old maxim that "one picture is worth more than ten-thousand words," because these days, "more than ten-thousand words are used to debate the worth of one picture."

Business men seem convinced that publicity pictures pay off. Many large corporations are now installing fully-equipped photo studios and laboratories in their headquarters to streamline their picture output as well as to improve its quality. Major news services such as Associated Press and United Press International have for some time serviced commercial clients through their subsidiary photo departments, and the steadily increasing demand for publicity pictures has made these subsidiaries highly successful ventures.

Among the nation's many and various communications media, there is an unmistakable trend toward the increased use of photographs. Photojournalism, as this comparatively new phase of journalism is called, is now generally accepted as a means for reporting current events, interpreting them and even analyzing them.

Life Magazine, one of the country's leading exponents of photojournalism, notes an enormous growth within the past twenty or thirty years in "the ability and willingness of Americans to look at pictures."

Joe Kastner, Copy Editor at *Life,* says that "over the

years, people are becoming more adept at appreciating and understanding pictures. We've had to hit the reader over the head with caption material less and less."

While the *New York Times* may continue to content itself with two modest pictures (one above and one below the fold) to accompany the news it sees fit to print on any average front page, many of its conservative colleagues in the United States are rapidly joining the ranks of the so-called "picture newspapers." *The New York Daily News,* with a staff of approximately fifty photographers, uses ninety pictures on an average day, as many as 114 on an unusual day. Recently the dignified *New York Herald Tribune* turned to using large pictures and many of them in an effort to increase circulation. To a degree, this approach has succeeded.

Many professionals credit television with making the American public more picture-conscious. They point out that since children begin viewing TV at a very tender age, their standards for pictures are automatically being set higher, and their appreciation of good pictures is more critical. This would tend to bear out the complaint of some parents that their children understand pictures better than they do words.

Get the Picture?

Nevertheless, despite the unblinkable fact that more and more pictures are being used these days, the value of these pictures in communicating an idea is still very much a subject for debate.

In an effort to shed some light on the situation, Bob Warner, Photo Editor of *Editor and Publisher* magazine, asked some of the nation's leading photojournalists these questions:

Are we as a nation more picture-conscious today than thirty or forty years ago?

Do readers appreciate good pictures, and do newspapers and magazines make big efforts to provide them?

Mr. Warner has been kind enough to let us share his findings with the readers of this book. They not only provide food for any man's thought, but they may also provide some clues for the part-time publicity chairman or full-time professional publicist who is trying to decide whether—and how far—to move into the publicity picture arena.

Cliff Edom, Professor of Photojournalism at the University of Missouri, takes a dim view of the real value of pictures as they are generally used today.

"Some people think we are a visual or picture-conscious nation," he says, "I don't think we are. We look at things and don't see them. We don't care what's in a picture as long as it's a gal in a bathing suit. After we see it, we don't spend much time with it. We don't give much credit to the photographer. We don't try to evaluate a picture.

"We've made surveys of the type of pictures we've used on our picture page at the *Columbia Missourian,* and we've found that it doesn't seem to make a great deal of difference whether it's feature material, whether it's old material or fresh, or even whether it's what we think is a fine picture. It's my interpretation that we have been brainwashed into thinking we like pictures, but as far as content is concerned, it makes little or no difference what is there."

Professor Edom concludes: "I would say that the general public is not at all critical of what types of pictures we have in our newspapers and magazines. I think they *could* know the difference between a good picture and a bad one, but they don't know it now."

Joseph Costa, chief photographer for King Features Syndicate, disagrees with Professor Edom.

"I don't think it's right," he says, "to expect the public to understand journalism to the point where they not only know what they like in a word-story picture, but can also analyze why they like it.

"A reader buys a particular newspaper because he likes what it prints, not because he has studied and compared word construction or literary style with other papers and then made a choice. Why should we ask readers to look at pictures with a critical eye which they haven't even brought to the older medium of words?

"Obviously, we can't expect readers to spend as much time studying pictures as they do reading words. In any case, they don't have to. One of the beauties of picture communication is that you don't have to look at a photograph for any appreciable length of time. The mental impressions come quickly; the idea a picture intends to get across hits the reader very rapidly."

Mr. Costa believes that publishers are becoming more and more picture-conscious and that quality will improve.

"Of course, some editors profess to have a great belief in the value of pictures but don't back up that claim with the kind of photo lab they need and the way in which their picture operation is run. This group, I believe, is in the minority. By and large, I think more and more editors every day are becoming more conscious of the needs of photojournalism and are willing to do something about it.

"Many publishers have attributed gains in circulation

96

to more picture coverage. Newspapers that didn't formerly use pictures at all brought an increase in circulation, revenue, and advertising when they reverted from non-use or meagre use of pictures."

This is a challenge that certainly will also confront the outsider in the communications field, the publicist and the publicity chairman who will be competing with the professionals of the working press for photo space in the newspapers.

For this reason, the remainder of this chapter has been designed to give both amateur and professional a clear and understandable guide to producing more effective publicity pictures.

Inviting the Photographer

Before you ask a newspaper for photo coverage, be sure that your meeting, convention or other event merits this kind of journalistic attention. Make your evaluation from the newspaper's point of view, not your own. This not only will make you a popular personality in the city room, but it will also avoid disappointments in your own camp.

Once you've decided your undertaking is of enough general interest to stand a chance in the race for newspaper space, extend your invitation, using the same "Press Memo" that you send to the city editor requesting a reporter's coverage.

This memo (also often called a "photo assignment tip") should reach the newspaper at least twenty-four hours in advance of the event. It should be sent—in most cases—to the picture editor. (On some very large papers, you may deal with photo assignment editor, in which case

news COMPANY NAME, ADDRESS AND PHONE NUMBER

FROM: YOUR NAME

TO: PHOTO EDITORS

DATE:

TIME:

PLACE:

SAMPLE PHOTO ASSIGNMENT TIP

you would still send a copy of the memo to the picture editor.)

Take time to telephone the newspaper for the correct name, spelling and title of the persons to whom you are sending your request. For details on what the press memo should contain and how it should look, see Chapter 7, "Accommodating the Press."

Accommodating the Photographer

Once your invitation for photo coverage has been accepted, be prepared to make the photographer's job as pleasant and easy as possible. Press photographers work against a deadline, and usually they have to shoot and run—either back to the office or on to another assignment immediately following yours.

If there are to be people in the picture (and there usually are) round them up well ahead of time. It's better to have your people wait around a bit than to run the risk of losing the photographer—or the photographer losing patience.

There is no need to panic, however, if the photographer shows up a few minutes before you're ready for him. It is only in rare instances that he will not shoot his assigned subject.

Well before the photographers arrive, prepare a special hand-out, giving the background of the event as well as the names of all the people involved. This will save time and will assure the accuracy of the caption that appears on the photo.

During the shooting of the picture, it is certainly permissible to suggest to the photographer any ideas you may have, but don't, under any circumstances, be insistent. Make your suggestion and then fade into the background.

99

Your handling of the photographer should be based upon simple courtesy and an understanding of his job. You need not feel you have to give him the red carpet treatment or any other special considerations to cajole his cooperation. If he's been assigned to cover the event, he'll get your picture. But he'll get a much better picture if you smooth the way for him, and you'll get much better cooperation all around the next time you invite photo coverage. For the additional necessary details on how to accomplish this, see Chapter 7, "Accommodating the Press."

Selecting Your Own Photographer

There are a number of good reasons why you should engage your own photographer to cover an event, even though the newspapers have agreed to cover it.

At the last minute, for instance, the man assigned to your event may have to be pulled off it and assigned to a late-breaking, more important story. In such a case, the editor may, when you call him, request that you take the picture and get it over to him.

Or, the photographer may arrive, shoot the picture, and then be directed to cover a four-alarm fire before he returns to the office. Your pictures may never get there in time for the early editions, or they may be sidetracked during processing to expedite the more pressing news pictures.

Photographers have been known to lose film holders, break legs or otherwise inconvenience the publicity man. Film has been known to be ruined in the processing. Be prepared. Have your own man on hand.

Don't, under any circumstances, "set up" a picture

situation primarily for the benefit of the press and then rely solely on the press to cover it.

The most astonishing instance of such naivete was provided by the paid, professional publicity director for a New York City youth group who complained that *three times* she had set up a picture of the Mayor with one of the children presenting a citation, and *three times* the press had failed to show!

(The publicity gal was most annoyed with the newspapers—and blankly surprised to learn that she should have had her own photographer on hand the *first* time for just such an eventuality.)

The Professional Touch

If your budget can stand it, hire a professional newsphoto service. As noted earlier in this chapter, news associations such as Associated Press and United Pres International provide complete publicity photo services. They will assign a photographer to cover your event and will have the picture taken, printed, captioned and on the desk of the newspaper editor within a few hours. Their photographers are usually former press photographers with a great deal of experience and skill in this area.

You might also check your local newspaper for a recommendation. Many large papers hire "stringers," photographers in various neighboring communities who cover special events for them on assignment and sometimes on a free-lance basis. These photographers usually have their own photo businesses and would welcome your assignment.

There are others in the publicity picture field—associations of photographers or individuals—who are equipped to cover your events, and many of them do fine work.

Picture editors complain, however, that many commercial processors are sloppy about the quality of their finished prints and often indifferent to deadlines.

Producing a good publicity photograph requires special skills and not every photographer can handle this assignment to the satisfaction of a picture editor. For a publicity picture to break into print, it must be something more than in focus. It must also convey an idea in a natural, journalistic style. With rare exceptions, the photographers of babies, weddings or proms cannot fill this order, nor can the photo hobbyist, however talented he may be.

Regardless of whom you persuade or hire to take your pictures, you as a publicist or publicity chairman should be well acquainted with certain basic rules of news photography. These will help you to work better with the good photographers and to direct the efforts of the other kind.

Taking the Picture

1. Pictures should be staged, not merely snapped. We do not mean by this that the picture should be a phony, but that it should be planned to tell a story or convey a message at a glance. This seldom happens if you try to catch your pictures on the fly.

2. News pictures should always include animate and active subjects—animals and/or people who are doing something. Don't allow your beauty contest winner to stand stiffly smirking at the camera. Have her admiring her prize, receiving her crown or showing it to others. Try to be as interesting as possible. By "interesting" we mean, if it weren't *your* picture, would you give it a second glance?

3. Subjects should always appear relaxed and as natural and pleasant as possible. Warning: No smile at all is better than one that is stiff and false.

4. Subjects should never stare directly into the camera lens. This gives the picture an artificial look and defeats the impression that you are recording news as it occurs. Give your subjects something to do, to hold, or to look at.

5. Where possible, avoid including more than two or three persons in one picture. Reduced in size for newspaper reproduction, an over-populated picture looks like a mob scene, the subjects are difficult to identify, the pose is usually dull, and the whole thing demands too much space on the news page. We know that usually every committee member wants to be included, but be firm on this point. If necessary, single out the newsmakers of the group for the photograph you will service to the paper. Then go ahead and take all the shots necessary to keep everyone happy. They can always go into your files and scrapbooks later.

6. A picture should be taken from more than one angle. Three shots of the same pose (close up, medium, long shot) or of the same subject in different poses give the editor variety to choose from. If you're lucky, if your prints are good and tell a story, you may break two, or possibly a "spread" of pictures in the paper.

7. Keep the background simple. Avoid busy, patterned wallpaper or jumbled activity in back of your subject. Make certain you don't have potted plants or birdcages growing out of someone's head.

8. Pay close attention to detail. Remove sun glasses which show up as black blobs. Remove all glasses, if possible, since they cause distracting reflections. At lunch-

eons, dinners, and parties, remove drinking glasses from your subjects' hands—unless, of course, you are photographing a toast. Make sure cigars and cigarettes are being held, not puffed.

9. Use lighting to make your pictures look interesting. Flat, full front, flash lighting produces flat, uninteresting prints. If you're using flash, and you cannot set up a second light some distance from the camera, hold the flash gun well away from the camera, high and to the right or left. This will give modeling to the subject. If you're shooting outdoors, use the sun in the same way— for sidelighting or backlighting. Either looks better than pictures in which the sun is behind the photographer and in the subjects' eyes.

10. Study the style of the pictures appearing in each newspaper you want to break. One may feature close-ups while another concentrates on detail and extensive backgrounds. Whenever possible, shoot each picture or pose with a specific paper in mind. This will help to improve your batting average considerably.

11. In a news photo, the subject matter should be timely and up-to-the-minute, showing well-known people (or unusually interesting unknowns) currently and actively involved in your event. Don't dredge up last year's picture, even if the subjects in it are the same. Picture editors have good memories.

Technical Requirements

1. Prints should be made on glossy paper, preferably the 8 x 10 size, never smaller than 5 x 7.

2. Avoid copy negatives (these are copies of an original print). In making prints, these negatives usually lose about 25 per cent of their original definition.

3. Prints should be sharp, perfectly in focus, with all grades of tones evident. Tones should span evenly from near-blacks (which contain detail, however) to medium and light greys. No burned-out whites, please.

4. Prints should not be cracked or bruised. Don't at any time write firmly on the back of the print, for this will crack the glossy finish on the print itself. When you write the names of the subjects and the date on the back, do so lightly, in ink. All imperfections in a print reproduce, and most newspapers will not take time to correct the print.

5. Pictures should not be retouched before they're sent to the newspaper. Save retouching for advertising matter or industrial pictures. If the print needs retouching, the editor will make the decision and have it done.

6. Crop your pictures before sending them in. Cropping is done to eliminate extraneous matter and provide as tight and interesting a picture as possible. The decision to crop should be made while you still have your proofs. (The professional photographer you hire should do this for you.)

Writing the Photo Caption

The photo caption, sometimes referred to as the "cutline," is a brief description of facts relevant to the picture. For some reason, the publicity man seems to take fewer pains with the photo caption than he does with the press release—and that's not many.

Picture editors complain that captions are sloppily presented and badly written, with cross-outs, inked-in insertions, changes and misspellings. One editor received a photo caption on which the typist's fingers were apparently out of position on the typewriter keys, and half the caption read like the hieroglyphics on an Egyptian cave.

The caption should list, clearly and factually, the following pertinent details:

1. Identification of the people in the picture, reading from left to right
2. Brief description of the action depicted
3. Brief summary of the event to which the picture pertains
4. Name, address, phone number of sending organization
5. Name and phone number of the sender (you, that is)

Keep the caption brief and factual. Let the action of the picture speak for itself. All the purple prose in the world cannot save a poor picture. Under normal circumstances, the actual copy should not run longer than four or five lines. If the editor wants more background information, he'll let you know soon enough.

(One picture editor requested that anyone sending in a photo also send him copy of the press release. This backstops him in the event a caption or picture is lost and fills in information he might need.)

The best way to learn caption writing is to study your daily newspaper. You will find that the caption information will vary little from paper to paper.

Preparing the Caption

When typing a caption, leave about three inches of blank space on the top. Then, with the copy facing out, lightly glue or tape the open top portion to the back of the picture itself. (Never join print and caption with a staple or paper clip.)

Fold the caption up over the print and slide it into an envelope where it is protected by one or more sheets of cardboard. When the editor removes the print, he can peel down the caption copy which will then appear directly under the picture itself.

7

ACCOMMODATING THE PRESS

OF ALL PRESS relations chores, none is so complex and demanding as that of accommodating the working press at a major special event. The moment you invite the press to cover an event—be it a main street parade or a testimonial dinner—you have taken on a responsibility that demands the most professional skills in handling press relations. Do it well, and your time and effort will be repaid in terms of good publicity coverage and the good will of the working press. Do it badly, and you would have been better off to have slept late or gone fishing.

Incompetent handling of the press at a special event can, at its worst, produce a fiasco of confusion and hard feeling and, at its least damaging, produce disappointing publicity coverage. Either may be disastrous, since newspaper publicity is usually the yardstick by which the success or failure of a special event is measured.

Long after the last marching band has tootled off into silence or the last laudatory speech has ended, those who sponsored the parade or the dinner (committee members and company executives alike) will pore over the publicity scrapbook, line by line, inch by inch, and clipping by clipping. Too often, by the time the book is closed, the clouds of disappointment have gathered to cast gloom over the entire undertaking.

Usually this is not the fault of the event itself, but of planners who did not plan well enough. For although many events are planned and produced expressly to garner publicity, the techniques for achieving this end often receive too little care and attention.

Yet with proper attention to the needs of the reporters and photographers on the job, most special events could become press publicity bonanzas. Naturally, the scope and newsworthiness of the event will determine the extent of the coverage you receive, but unless you plan properly, you cannot hope to reap the full publicity harvest of your undertaking.

This chapter deals with the specific techniques involved in helping the newspaperman do his job in the most comfortable and efficient manner possible. This, of course, will not "guarantee" coverage in the papers—nothing in the chancey world of newspapering is guaranteed—but it will assure you a better-than-fighting chance and certainly a receptive attitude next time around.

Assuming that your event is newsworthy and merits the attention of the press, you should be equipped to prepare and handle: The press memo, press room, transportation, press table, special interviews, press conference, the press party, and the press kit.

The Press Memo

There are many ways to invite press coverage of a special event. Some publicists just pick up the telephone; some drop in on the editor; still others send telegrams. These methods might get results in a pinch, but when you're inviting coverage of a special event, you should not be "in a pinch."

For one thing, as we have mentioned earlier and often, a telephone call or a personal visit is sure to annoy a busy editor. A telegram is fine when your message is urgent and timely, but this should not be the case with a press invitation. Your event should be planned well enough in advance to allow comfortable timing.

The accepted method of invitation is the "press memo." (This is true no matter what kind of event you're staging.) It is as acceptable to the editor of the business page or woman's page as it is to the city editor.

The press memo can be mimeographed on the standard 8½ x 11 sheet of white bond paper. It should look like this:

TO: CITY DESK
                     PHOTO DESK
                     (Or Appropriate Department)

FROM: JOHN JONES (Title)
                     Name of company or organization
                     Address
                     Telephone and extension for John Jones

SUBJECT: GRAND OPENING OF (name of store, park, etc.)

DATE: SATURDAY, OCTOBER 3, 1962

TIME: 10 A.M.

PLACE: IN FRONT OF MAIN ENTRANCE, NORTH SIDE (Address) *

DESCRIPTION: Describe the activity planned, the names of speakers, etc.

(*Note: If event is being held out of town and special transportation is available to the press, include all details on the memo.)

Instead of a press memo, many publicity people send a copy of their press release with the added notation: "Inviting press coverage." This is not as effective. If the brief description that appears on the memo does not adequately cover the event, include a press release WITH the memo.

Timing the Invitation

Send out your invitations in time to allow an editor to assign a reporter (and a photographer) to cover. Don't wait until the last minute, but don't send the invitation too early, either. An editor seldom assigns a reporter or photographer far in advance of the day of the event.

The reason for this is obvious. A newspaper is in the business of covering the news as it occurs, not anticipating it. Most assignments are made from day to day, or possibly a day in advance, and an editor tries at all times to keep his staff assignments flexible. There is enough taking place from day to day—and hour to hour—to keep a news staff on its toes.

Some editors may put a very early announcement in what they call the "future file," but more often, they just file them in the wastebasket.

When you are dealing with the city desk, *send out your press memo about three days before the event if it is of local origin.* If it is taking place out of town, send out the invitation a week ahead of time.

When you are dealing with specialized departments such as the woman's page, business page and others, allow for less flexibility on the editor's part, since the staffs here are usually small. *Allow about one week for local events and up to two more weeks for events out of town.*

Timing the Event

Since most special events are planned for their publicity value, publicity considerations generally govern the date selected. (For example, you would not set a date that conflicts with other news-making events in the community and thus force yourself to compete for valuable newspaper space.)

Of equal (possibly greater) importance to the publicist or the publicity chairman is the hour at which the event takes place. Here, newspaper deadlines should be given top priority in planning, for no matter how unusual the event or how large the turnout, if you've missed the newspapers' editions, you've missed the boat.

Generally speaking, the earlier in the day an event takes place, the better are your chances of breaking into print. This is particularly true of the morning papers. But for both morning and afternoon papers, 10 a.m. is generally regarded as an excellent hour.

It allows reporters and photographers to cover, to get back to their offices, to write the story (or develop the pictures) in time to make the early editions comfortably. Don't forget that at a special event you are holding the press for an unusual length of time and may even be drawing them out of town. Thus time, for you, plays a major role in the success or failure of the event.

There are occasions, of course, when there is nothing you can do about the hour. If, for instance, the event is an evening affair—a dinner or a dance—you will just have to take your chances.

Advance Story

One way to better your odds and service the morning

papers at the same time is to prepare an "advance" story. Include this with your press memo.

The advance story should cover the general news of the event, such as the background, the program planned, the speakers expected, and other factors that are likely to remain unchanged. Be very careful with details, however. With special events, anything can happen (and usually does) to change the course of the program or the evening, thus making your advance story inaccurate.

Generally speaking, however, an advance story should protect you for the early editions of the morning papers. If something really newsworthy or unusual comes out of the event, the reporter who covers can turn in a more detailed story for the later editions.

Follow-Up

The day before your event, call the newspapers to determine approximately how many reporters and photographers will attend. This should not annoy an editor. In fact, it will serve to back-stop him, in case he has forgotten the event or lost your press memo. It also will help you to adjust your accommodations. You may need more staff or material for a better-than-anticipated turn-out, or, you may have to cut down liquor and food requirements if the turn-out is small.

Make one final call on the morning of the event.

This will serve as one last reminder to the editor. Better still, it may provide you with an opportunity to service him. Since late-breaking news has no regard for schedules or assignment sheets, reporters and photographers, often at the last minute, may be taken off your event and reassigned to another, more pressing story. In such cases, the editor may ask you to cover for him.

113

Dinner Anyone?

When you invite representatives of the press to a dinner or a luncheon, send them the same invitation that is sent all other guests and attach to it a "MEMO TO THE EDITOR."

This memo should contain all the information that appears in the press release (see Chapter 5) plus the following information:

1. A list of dais guests
2. A list of speakers, with a notation indicating which speeches will be available in advance copies
3. Time and place of reception, if one is planned
4. This line: "TABLES HAVE BEEN SET ASIDE FOR THE PRESS"

The Press Table

While a press "room" is a must for outdoor events and large indoor functions, a press table or tables will suffice for newspaper people at luncheons, dinners and banquets. The size and number of tables depend entirely upon how many press invitations have been accepted.

The press table should be placed as close as possible to the speakers' table or dais, and at the same time, near an exit. This will allow reporters and photographers to make discreet departures when they are satisfied they have enough information and pictures.

The table should be clearly marked, "PRESS" and should be hosted by members of the publicity committee or the publicity department. They will supply newsmen with press kits and handouts from a well-stocked reservoir close at hand. Needless to say, they will also pick up all the checks for refreshments.

114

Be sure they know the location of the nearest telephone so that they can direct members of the press to it, if necessary.

Before the luncheon begins, arrange with the head waiter to impress upon waiters assigned to the press table the importance of good and attentive service there.

Also make certain that the press table is clearly indicated on the seating plan and that all receptionists know precisely where it is located. This is important, since at any luncheon or dinner program, all table numbers and identifications come down once waiters begin to serve the meal. A late-arriving member of the press can quickly become lost (and annoyed) among the hundreds of tables and thousands of guests that any large ballroom accommodates.

The Press Room

The press "room" is a specific gathering place for reporters and photographers and is an essential accommodation when you are staging an outdoor event (such as a parade or street fair) or a large indoor event (such as a convention).

It may be a room in a hotel, store, or office; or it may not be a room at all, but a station wagon, a trailer, a truck, or a booth on a street corner. Whatever it is, it should be clearly marked: "FOR PRESS ONLY" and should be placed as close as possible to the locale of the event.

The press room should be staffed by members of your publicity committee or department, and these people should be prepared to assist the newsmen in every way — running errands, holding lights and ladders, making phone calls, providing essential materials.

115

These should include a substanial stack of press releases, press kits and hand-outs. The hand-out is a press release that includes last-minute changes or information not included with other press material. It MUST be handed to every photographer and reporter covering the event. It provides a quick, brief, recapitulation of the goings-on when things are moving too fast for referral to other, more comprehensive material. The late-arriving newsman usually asks for the handout before he takes his hat off.

In addition to printed materials, the press room should also provide the basic tools of a working newsman's trade, namely:

1. Chairs and tables
2. Typewriters and plenty of paper
3. Telephones
4. Pads and pencils
5. Ladders for the photographer (for better camera angles)
6. Errand boys and girls (any age)

Almost as essential as the above are plenty of hot coffee, sandwiches, hard or soft drinks. You'll have to be prepared to be strict about the "press only" ruling, since this is an area that exerts a strong fascination for workers, volunteers and interested bystanders.

Special Interviews

Special interviews are exceedingly difficult to arrange while an event is in progress. If an editor or covering reporter wants a private chat with some particular person involved in the event (such as guest speaker, company executive), try to get them together immediately after the event or during the day before. Those hours preceding

116

and during the event will demand the undivided attention of all participants. To cut into this time for an interview not only can disrupt the proceedings, but also can produce an unsatisfactory interview so far as the newsman is concerned.

No matter when the interview has been scheduled, once it is set, attach yourself firmly and unshakeably to the interviewee. Often in the excitement of an event, such committments are innocently forgotten. It will be your job to remember.

Transportation

Be prepared to transport members of the press to and from your event and throughout its duration as well. If your project takes place outside the city proper, arrange a press shuttle service (bus or automobile) to run at regular intervals from convenient, designated points to the event locale. When you are transporting large groups of newspaper people (on a bus, for instance) see to it that they are accompanied by a competent publicity person who can answer questions en route, handle special requests and generally be of all-around usefulness.

Provide restricted parking facilities near the press room for newsmen driving their own cars. Be sure to notify gate guards of such arrivals and authorize their entry.

When an event is spread over a wide area, as in the case of parades, fairs and other outdoor events, have cars available to take reporters and photographers to the various points of interest.

A note caution: If you are lucky enough to have motion picture people on hand as well as still photographers — keep them apart! The needs of motion picture photographers for television and newsreels are entirely different from the needs of newspaper photographers. During major events, the conflict between these two media creates a monumental headache for the publicity man in charge.

Avoid this by preparing for it. Assign separate facilities and personnel to each group.

The Press Conference

A press conference is a special meeting called for the purpose of making announcements of great importance to representatives of all newspapers at the same time. Its value as a publicity tool is debatable at best, and it should be used only after thoughtful deliberation.

Press conferences often are called to make announcements that could just as easily have been covered in routine press releases. When this happens, press relations suffer. Newspapermen don't relish investing time and shoe leather unnecessarily; and you can be sure the editor will hear about it.

These questions can help you determine whether a press conference is necessary:

1. Is the announcement of great news value?
2. Is a routine press release inadequate to cover all the information?
3. Is the announcement complicated enough to require additional explanation by specialists?
4. Is it controversial enough to be misinterpreted unless it is discussed in detail with reporters?

If you can answer "yes," to the above questions, a press conference may be justified.

It should take place in the offices of the company calling the conference. The board room, chief executive's office, or any other room big enough and private enough for such a meeting will suffice.

If you anticipate a large press turn-out, arrange the room in theater fashion, with chairs facing the front of the room where staff members will be seated at a long table. At a small press conference, reporters and company officials can work effectively around the table, as in a board meeting.

Only executives qualified to speak for the organization (the chief executive officer, public relations director) should represent the company at the meeting. If the conference is called to discuss technical matters as well as policy, have present representatives of each division involved to deal with technical questions.

A press conference should start and end promptly at the hours announced. The highest ranking officer customarily presides over the meeting, referring to members of the staff questions he cannot adequately answer.

If the room is very large and presents an acoustical problem, it is advisable to provide microphones for the speakers and members of the press.

A word of caution: If you are not prepared or disposed to face a barrage of questions (some of which might prove delicate or embarrassing) , shun a press conference. Nothing is more frustrating to members of the working press than being summoned to interview someone who suddenly turns coy. Remember, you invited them. You have an obligation to "come clean."

The best rule to follow is: When in doubt about calling a press conference — don't.

The Press Party

The press party or reception (sometimes confused

with the press conference, but not even a sixth cousin) is an occasion at which the press is entertained while being exposed to a special interest of the host organization. A press party can introduce a new product, a new design, a new store, new ideas, a person or groups of persons, or it can simply say "thank you," for past courtesies.

The press party can be a happy affair, since it makes no pretense of being important and breeds none of the tensions so often found in press conferences. So long as the food and drink are plentiful and the service is good, a press party can create only good will. After all, everyone likes a good party, newspapermen possibly a little more than most.

However, good food and good service are not enough to warrant a full press turn-out. There must be a sound reason for the party. For example, an important diplomat arrives from Washington; a well-known movie star arrives from Hollywood to participate in activities attending a special event. A press party can introduce the celebrities to the press and, at the same time, introduce the press to the details of the event.

The press party is also an excellent way to preview an event before it is officially and publicly launched. Trade shows, merchandise sales, exhibits or entertainment programs can be successfully previewed this way. Newsmen can eat and then be given an unimpeded tour or watch a show in pleasant and relaxed circumstances.

Like the press conference, the press party is given for all newspapers at once and is timed to coincide with the news impact of some special announcement or event. That is, it should take place not a month, or even a week, before, but only a day or two in advance so that the memory of the party is still fresh when the event or announcement occurs.

A press party can be given at an appropriate restaurant or hotel or in the company's offices or plant — in which case it should be professionally catered. The site should be selected with the convenience of newsmen in mind. Natuarally, if the party celebrates the opening of a new store or plant, it should take place on the premises.

Schedule such a party within the luncheon or cocktail hours. You should not cut too deeply into the working day, nor should you interfere with commuters' schedules and dinner time.

One more word: If the party is to be held at the plant or, at any rate, some distance from town, be sure to provide transportation. (See section on transportation earlier in this chapter.)

The Press Kit

A press kit is a collection of all the vital statistics of a special event. Assembled in a folder or special envelope, this material presents every conceivable kind of information about the people, places and things involved in the event. Handed out to members of the press at such functions as the press conference and press party, or available in quantity in the press room, the press kit should provide an invaluable packet of information and background data for reporters.

The following materials usually are included in the kit:

1. Copies of all press releases sent out to date
2. Additional stories covering other aspects of the event
3. A short history of the sponsoring organization

4. Thumbnail fact sheet giving brief technical and informational data about the organization, its products, floor space, participants, costs, etc.

5. Agenda: A blow-by-blow time schedule of the event, (or series of events) from National Anthem to Benediction

6. Guest list

7. Copies of all speeches

8. Copies of luncheon or dinner menus

9. Detailed biographies of the important members of the sponsoring group: Officers, managers, volunteers

10. Properly-captioned photographs of important members of the sponsoring organization: Volunteers, speakers, entertainers, the plant or store, products, product applications.
(See Chapter 6, "Working With Pictures and the Photo Desk.")

Some organizations take great pains in designing the press kit covers, employing colorful art work and lettering on unusual envelopes, boxes or cases. This is fine if you can afford it, but don't forget that the most important part of a press kit is the material it contains.

The press kit is also useful in special mailings to newspapers. This, however, is not recommended for broadside distribution but only for selected occasions such as when a newspaper is preparing a special section on a subject in which you have a vested interest. A full kit from an automobile parts manufacturer, for example, would be most welcome to the editor of a special automobile section.

A press kit is also appreciated at weekly newspapers

and trade journals whose editors are constantly in need of material in depth.

Tips 'n' All

We have included a section on gratuities in this chapter because many publicity people still believe that a well-timed gift to an editor or reporter is part of accommodating the press.

Nothing could be further from the truth.

Although the practice of giving gifts to newspaper people is widespread, its value is questionable. With few exceptions, a gift — "payola," to be blunt — seldom produces preferential treatment for the giver. Quite often it produces annoyance or resentment.

Many newspapers have laid down a policy of returning all gifts. Many editors and reporters have adopted similar policies on their own initiative. On some papers, a dollar value is placed on the gifts, and the expensive ones are returned. The payola problem is most flagrant at Christmas time when many a city room takes on the appearance of the shipping department at Gimbels or Macy's.

Frequently, the case of liquor, basket of fruit or especially prepared cake is not used by the person it is sent to, but passed around the department instead — and usually without due credit to the sender. Many editors do not even look at the name of the sender before the passing-around begins.

There is no doubt, however, that some payola pays off. In any business enterprise, there is always one man — a purchasing agent, a buyer, a department head — who demands payment for services rendered. The newspaper business is no exception.

The practice of sending gifts is a matter of personal philosophy. A gift can be a friendly reminder that you are around. It also can offend the recipient. Approach any gift-giving thoughtfully.

8

WORKING WITH
THE BUSINESS PAGE

To A publicity man servicing business news, the Business Page is the most important department of any newspaper. Unlike the "city side" which uses stories of general interest, the business page talks directly to the select audience most firms want to reach. And, unlike many other departments, the business department extends to the publicist a courteous, even warm reception.

This is because the publicity man specializing in the complex and highly diversified field of business and finance has a unique value to the business page editor. The matter of company earnings is a classic example. Obviously, the editor cannot ask to see the company's books, so he depends, instead, upon the publicity representative to provide that information fully and accurately.

Donald I. Rogers, Business and Financial Editor of *The New York Herald Tribune,* says frankly:

"I believe the public relations man performs a useful function. If we tried to cover the field ourselves, we would need a staff of several hundred people, and we still wouldn't have a staff familiar with all the corporate officers and their individual problems. The job is too big."

The publicity man in this field, therefore, is actually

an extension of the newspaper staff — paid, to be sure, by the company or firm he represents, but providing the business page with its most valued commodity — news.

As the *Tribune's* Mr. Rogers points out:

"The publicity man who covers an industry is quite valuable to us because he possesses the technical knowledge and background information we need. I feel no compunction about letting a public relations man relay our questions to the top man in his company. If they give us a phony answer, we'll print it as it stands and clobber them with it."

This willingness of the business page staff to work with publicity men has not, to date, spared business page editors who have the same problems with publicists as do editors of other departments — with a few unique problems thrown in.

The press releases that come to the business page are just as badly presented, poorly executed and sloppily written as those going to other departments of the paper. But, to make matters worse, many press representatives in the business field play hard to get when a reporter is seeking information.

To anyone who has been pounding on editorial doors for any length of time, this may seem an exaggeration, but business editor after business editor has voiced the same complaint.

The managing editor of one the country's most respected newspapers summed it up this way:

"Business men are surrounded by a wall of press agents that keeps the editors from primary news sources. The motto of some press relations' staffs seems to be, 'We'll give you anything but information.' "

It goes without saying that any press representative

who is preoccupied with keeping the press outside the company doors is dissipating his opportunities and performing a disservice to his company. The same is true of those who have not taken the trouble to learn the needs of the business page and its editor. For although the business editor may welcome the publicity man's information and be more than willing to cooperate with him, he has no time to give courses in instant journalism to men who are paid to know better.

The Business Editor

The editor of the average business page is more than an experienced journalist; he is also something of an expert on the affairs of industry, commerce and finance. He must have an understanding of the behind-the-scenes operations of the stock market, the profit and loss picture of the country's leading corporations, and an insight into the politics of their personnel changes.

The business editor directs a staff of journalists who are specialists in various fields of business endeavor: Retailing, the stock market, railroads, banking, advertising, and others. It is their responsibility to understand at least one — generally two or three — areas, and through a variety of techniques to keep abreast of the news in all of them every day.

The size and scope of the job is apparent in one glance at the range of business and financial news that is covered daily on the business page of a large daily paper. This will include utilities, transportation, retailing, oil and chemicals, communications, automotive, advertising, banking and finance, the stock market. Newspapers like *The Herald Tribune, The New York Times* and *The Wall Street Journal* have more than the usual business page problems, since they publish in New York City, "the home office of the nation" and site of the country's two largest stock exchanges.

Many other newspapers throughout the country, however, also cover business news in depth. For the publicity man whose job is serving business clients, or for the executive who has been assigned to report his company's news to the press, here is a breakdown of the industries and activities that belong on the average business page.

Utilities

All public utilities such as gas, light and water. Routine news in this field includes earnings reports, construction of plants and other facilities, introduction of new processes and services, the movements of executives and introduction of new personnel policies. Stories of new products stand a chance here, providing, of course, they fit neatly into this category.

Transportation

Railroads, bus lines, airlines and trucking. (Marine transportation is usually handled in its own special section.) Routine news in this field consists of earnings and revenue reports (passenger and freight revenues), as well as changes in schedules, new routes, mergers, changes of fares, new facilities and movement of executives.

Retailing

Major or minor department stores, specialty shops, discount houses, shopping centers, buying offices (local, national and foreign) and small retail shops. Sales is the important news in this category; not just sales as income but also of the volume of sales of specific products and departments. Retail news stories also include such special events as openings, sales, anniversary celebrations, new display ideas, executive changes and additions. Note: Here is one area where, if the store is important in the community and the special event is big enough, it might make a story for the city side, so keep both city desk and business page alerted.

Oils and Chemicals

Production is the most important news in the oil industry followed by prices and new product development. Stories in this area might also stem from the opening and closing of facilities, diversification of production, earnings reports and mergers, the movement of executives and special events with a strong community flavor.

Communications

The field of electronic data processing, radio and television (business only, not programming or personalities) , telephone and telegraph. News here would be development of new communication devices, systems and processes, new facilities and products, earnings reports and mergers, executive movements and community events.

Automotive

The automobile industry is one of the largest single industries in the United States, and the economy of the country is affected by and reflected in its activities and progress. The business page is looking for more than style trends in new models. It wants anticipated car production and sales, new facilities and product diversification, profit and loss, dividend statments, new selling concepts and advance outlooks, and executive movements. Here, the individual new and used car dealer or garage operator is out in the cold unless he has some strong and unusual business news.

Advertising

In New York City, the advertising columnists have avid followings. Their columns cover the field of public relations as well as marketing, merchandising, publishing and the graphic arts. The big story here will concern the appointment of an advertising or public relations agency to handle a particular account. The bigger the account in size, prestige and billings, the bigger the story. If an account moves from one agency to another or changes personnel within the company, the paper will want to know the reasons behind the switch, the billings involved, and the story behind the personnel changes. Other advertising news includes new campaigns, developments in radio and television, advertising budgets, circulation figures, and the usual personnel changes.

Metals

Steel and other important metals usually are handled by one reporter who is a specialist in his field. Aside from the usual company reports and announcements, the publicity man representing a metals firm should be prepared to assist the reporter in developing industry stories on price trends, production, new processes, mining operations, and so forth. The publicity man's reward for this work usually is a prominent mention for his company.

Banking

Stories in this area are primarily technical discussions of money, money, money. These might be news of mortgage rates, interest rates, discount rates on loans. Some business pages also cover such areas as public relations practices among banks, community activities, drive-in windows, and so forth.

Publicity Pitfalls

With so broad a field to cover and with such diversity of industries, it is easy to understand why business page editors are always looking (and hoping) for an articulate, well-informed and professional publicity man.

Still, the unhappy truth is that the business publicity man makes many of the same mistakes that the publicity chairman of the local garden club does. The business editor echoes the lament of all other department editors: Most of the publicity material he gets is poorly conceived and badly executed.

Donald Rogers, veteran business and financial editor of *The New York Herald Tribune,* has been exposed to the workings of the business publicity man as much as, or more than, any business editor in the country. He cites these common examples of poor publicity servicing:

Phony Stories

"So many business publicity stories are predicated on one thing — to sell their product or one of their company executives — and publicity men will phony-up a story to bring this out. Too often they invent news to get an executive's name in the paper, instead of getting it in as a result of news. I keep a sort of mental black list of publicity men who have fed us information which has proved to be inaccurate or misleading. I can be tricked — but only once."

Undue Pressure

"So many public relations men think they are the only ones who call my office. They call to say they are sending a release, then they call to ask if it got here, then they call and ask if we are going to use it. Some of them even go as as far as to call up and ask, 'Did you use the story? I don't take the Trib.'

"Every day 800 to 1,500 pieces of mail addressed to me personally arrive at my office. Each and every one is opened, read, distributed, and handled in the way we see fit. In addition, from 3:00 to 6:00 P.M. daily, our busiest time, I receive more than eighty phone calls.

"You can readily see why, when a publicity man calls up to ask if I got his release, I get a little irate."

Mr. Rogers offers this advice: "A story is a story. It will stand on its own feet. If it has merit we will use it. We don't need pressure from publicity men. Their calls just take up time that could be used to read and process their releases.

"There are always good stories that don't get in, of course, because of time and space factors. But we try to read every piece of mail we get and give it some consideration."

Lack of Understanding

"My biggest complaint is that many publicity people don't bother to find out how the people on the firing line earn their living.

"An unbelievable number of times, the professional publicity man will call me to ask what is the best way or the best day of the week to get a story in the paper. When I have to take time to answer this question, I'm performing the expert's job that they are getting big salaries to perform." (Mr. Rogers points out there is no "best time" to call. The worst time, however, is deadline time.)

"Why don't they bother to learn the technicalities of being an editor and working under the pressures of time? They don't seem to realize that when we have done a story on a certain subject, it is covered. We can't keep doing the same story over and over just because their client had something he wants to add."

Poor Writing

"I wish publicity men would stop trying to be Hemingways. All we want them to do is to put the facts down on paper clearly and concisely and mail it to us. We'll put the 'writing' in and ask for more facts if we need them."

Servicing

"It is not necessary to come in in person with the release — that just eats up the time."

Discourtesy

"Some publicity people seem even to lack common courtesy. That's why I have to have an unlisted telephone at my home and lie about my whereabouts sometimes. They call me at home, on my vacation and even when I was in the hospital."

Encouraging Note

"As a group, however, I believe the publicity man does perform a vital function and with a very high degree of ethics."

In successfully performing this "vital function," every business publicity man will be obliged to handle certain basic news stories. These will vary, depending upon whether they concern a private firm or a publicly-owned corporation. Some are unique to neither group, since both can make news with a grand opening, plant expansion program or a new product.

A publicly-owned corporation, however, has more news potential than a private firm, since it discharges its responsibility to its public by means of stockholder meetings, dividend statements and earnings reports — all grist to the mill of the business page.

Handling this kind of news requires experience if it is to satisfy the business editor.

Here, as in other areas, the press release is the primary tool of the publicity man. The techniques for preparing a press release for the business page are no different than for other departments of the paper. However, the contents will vary and their handling by the business editor will be considerably different from the handling by the city desk.

How much of your release is used, or whether it will be used at all, depends upon factors entirely out of your control, factors such as space restrictions or an unusual volume of material. Often a story will get as far as being set in type and then will wind up in the "overset." Sometimes, stories in the overset can be updated and used, but more often, they are too old, and are by then outnumbered by newer stories.

Keep your stories brief and to the point. For some reason, publicity men seem to feel that business news is wordy news, and many a business press release will run from four to ten pages in length. This verbiage is all right for impressing someone in the company, but it will get you nowhere except in the doghouse with the business page staff.

Competition for space on the business page is keen, and there is little you can do to improve your chances over other stories. The story will have to stand on its own. We are not so naive, however, that we can overlook the personal element in publicity placement. Once in a while, a very good contact or friend on the paper may get you a break on a not-so-very-good story, but you can use this avenue only once—twice at the most. Then you'll have to go back to digging up really newsworthy items that deserve to be printed.

(For details on the preparation of press releases see Chapter 5.)

Any comprehensive coverage of business news will include these stories:

Stock market column
Executive appointments
Annual meetings
Earnings reports
Dividends
Plant expansion and construction
New products
Grand openings
Mergers
Speeches
Stock tables
Bonds

Stock Market Column

Rarely will the publicity man be called upon to work with the writer on the stock market column. This daily report of trading on the New York Stock Exchange is probably the most important news on the financial page, and it is usually written by a reporter who has become an expert stock analyst. It is his job to interpret the market action for his readers.

It is a good idea to send copies of your press releases to him, however, for they frequently provide background material for stories that break in this area. They also help him to make an accurate analysis of the performance of the company's stock.

Sometimes, the writer of this column, in watching the ticker, will notice some unusual action. A company's stock may jump suddenly from $25 a share to $28. The reporter will then get on the phone and find out from a broker what is going on. If what is going on is the rumor of a merger or some other company action, he will tip off the business editor who will then assign another reporter to check out the rumor.

Here is where you can do your company a service or a disservice depending upon whether you decide to shield the company president from the queries of the press or to deal frankly with reporters.

If your company doesn't want to comment — say so. This, at least, will give the reporter a concrete fact for his story: "Executives at the VCA Company declined to comment on the rumor."

Whatever you do, answer the telephone. Don't try to duck a reporter. He'll get his story anyway, and you will have missed the opportunity to see that your company's viewpoint is fairly represented. (See Chapter 4, "Working With the City Desk.")

Executive Appointments

These appointments are announced to the papers through the press release which may be accompanied by a picture of the executive.

If your company has elected a president, a chairman of the board, a director, or a vice-president, the news will usually rate a picture and a caption-story. (If a major company is involved, i.e., Standard Oil or du Pont, the story may rate fuller treatment.)

But if your new executive is below the level of vice president, chances are his picture will not get much "play." Such lower-ranking appointments are usually lumped together in one column or story, with each appointment graded according to importance. Half-column pictures of the four most important men on the list may be used to illustrate this column.

If you have elected new directors, their names will be news. The re-election of the old board members is not.

If you do include a picture of the newest appointee, write his name and the name of the company on the back of the picture — lightly, though, so as not to mar the print. (See Chapter 6, "Working with Pictures.") Even once-properly captioned pictures have a way of getting separated from copy in the sorting and handling of mail, and if there is no way to identify your man, he will wind up in the wastebasket.

Annual Meetings

Most companies hold their annual meetings at about

137

the same time of year — usually in the Spring. This means that for two or three weeks out of the year, newspapers are flooded with the reports of annual meetings. Even if only a paragraph were devoted to each company, these reports could take up two or three columns of news space. The editor, therefore, must be selective and boil down the reports he does use to a brief paragraph or two.

This Spring flood also means that the editor cannot possibly assign a reporter to cover every meeting, and must depend upon you, the publicity man, to get the information to him. Your press release should include any important action that has been taken — such as the election of officers, the approval of a stock split, or a forecast of next year's business, an estimate of this year's sales and earnings.

Annual meetings of such industry leaders as U.S. Steel, General Motors, General Electric, probably will be covered by a reporter since these companies' plans, sales and profit prospects are indications of what an entire industry can expect.

Even if a reporter covers the meeting, however, be prepared to provide him with copies of speeches, financial reports, proxy material and any other prepared material that can help him write a better story.

Earnings Reports

Since most companies operate on the calendar year, their earnings statements usually are issued at the same time, and within the space of a week, newspaper offices can be buried under hundreds of earnings reports. This means that unless your company is of major importance or reports exceptionally large profits (or, heaven forbid, losses) , it will probably find itself with dozens of other companies cozily nestled together under one headline.

Usually the editor will group like businesses together — all the drug companies in one story, railroads, airlines, utilities in others, and those that do not fit neatly into any pigeonhole lumped together.

Regardless of what treatment you can logically expect at the hands of an editor, your press release on the company earnings report should include certain basic information: (a) Profits (or net earnings or net income) , and (b) gross sales or net sales, (c) comparative figures for previous year.

Other details will depend upon the kind of company you work for.

If your company manufactures machine tools or heavy industrial equipment, you should include the backlog of unfilled orders as compared to the same period a year ago.

A report for oil producers should include average daily production totals.

Transportation companies should include passenger and freight volume.

Steel and other metal producers should note the operating rate in relation to plant capacity.

It is important to include an explanation for substantial increases or decreases in sales or profits. For instance, you might note that "profits are off because of heavy research and development costs," or "sales are up because of the acquisition of a new company."

Your report might also include an account of important company developments in the past year — acquisitions, mergers, sale of property, a large tax refund, new

products. And it can include management's opinion of
the outlook for the coming year.

Dividends

Reports of dividend actions are legitimate, routine
news for the business page, but the only source of such
news is the company press release. This might be issued
to announce:

    a. Changes in the quarterly dividend rate
    b. Special cash or stock dividend
    c. Payment of stock dividend in lieu of cash
    d. An explanation of why the action was taken

The declaration of the regular quarterly dividend is
considered news, but will usually be printed along with
many others in a column of agate (5-½ point) type. On
the other hand, if a company omits payment of a dividend
or pays its usual dividend in spite of a drop in profits, the
story will be major news.

Plant Expansion and Construction

A story of the construction of a factory, warehouse,
office building, store or laboratory has approximately
three chances to make the business page of a newspaper:

    a. When plans for construction are announced
    b. When construction begins
    c. When it is completed

A story about the expansion of existing facilities has
two chances: When it is planned and when it is completed.

Certain basic information should be included in your
press release on both kinds of stories:

    a. The cost of the construction or expansion

b. The date the work will begin and the date it will be completed

c. The size of the new plant or addition, in square feet, in the number of stories, or in area, i.e., three blocks, 75 acres

d. The location

There will be other descriptive information which is appropriate and meaningful to a particular industry. You might want to say something about the financing arrangements or add the name of the architect or contractor.

IMPORTANT: Be sure to include information about the purpose of the new plant or addition. That is, if it is a manufacturing plant, what will it manufacture? What will be its annual capacity? What will the products be used for? Is it a new product or a new manufacturing endeavor for the company? If it is a new office building or distribution center, tell the editor what company departments will be housed in it. If it's a store, tell what it will sell and what effect it will have on profits and sales.

Be sure to explain where the new plant or store fits into the company's present facilities.

If the amount of money involved in the expansion or construction is high in the millions, or if the planned expansion represents a new activity for the company, it may rate a separate story on the business page, and possibly even a picture. On the other hand, it may rate only a paragraph by itelf, or be included in a collection of stories appearing under one general head.

The names of the men who have been appointed to important positions in the new store or plant may be included in the release.

Mergers

News of the sale of a company or of some of its assets or property to another company usually appears on the business page in a story which covers a number of such actions. The most important story will be given the "lead," with other stories following in order of descending importance.

If the transaction involves a major company or an unusually large amount of money, the story may be handled separately.

Your press release about the merger should include the following information:

a. Names and identifying information about each of the companies involved. This should include annual sales, total assets, principal products, annual profit, number of employees, historical background.

b. Terms of the merger. The sale price and the method of payment are most important to the financial page editor and should be given whenever possible. When the company chooses not to disclose the terms of the agreement, the release should say so. If any partial information is given, the release might state: "The purchase was made for an undisclosed amount of cash and stock." If the terms are disclosed, they should be given in detail: the exact amount of cash or the number of shares involved in a stock exchange; the price of the stock, the number of shares outstanding, the rate of exchange.

c. Plans for the operation of the acquired company. Your release should include information about the future operation of the acquired company and any changes in management. It should state whether the company will be operated as a division, a subsidiary or whether it will be absorbed into the other company. Changes in the company name also should be reported.

d. Reason for merger. If possible, include in your release a statement from the president of one or both of the companies about the reasons for, and advantages of, the merger. This might be: to diversify into a new field, to acquire a supplier company, to expand retail outlets, to promote the development of a certain product, and so forth.

New Products

Some papers publish a new products column in which miscellaneous product publicity can be placed. Sometimes this appears on the business page and sometimes in another section of the paper.

Often, a new product or a new process can have a profound effect upon a company's sales and profits, and thereby would rate separate treatment on the business page. In such a case, the story might also be accompanied by a picture.

If you do send a picture to the business page, however, don't make the mistake of thinking that cheesecake will sell it. The boys on the copy desk will enjoy it, but the readers will never have the pleasure. A barely-clad maiden holding a trip-hammer will never appear on the business page.

This does not mean that you can't use people in a product publicity picture. Even a pretty girl, suitably clothed, can make the financial page if she is demonstrating a new typewriter or telephone switchboard.

Grand Openings

Stories of this kind fall roughly into the same category as plant expansion and construction stories. Most editors will, at the very least, acknowledge the fact of a grand opening with a paragraph or two. If the story is more important, they may run a separate story with a picture. Offer the editor enough material for a good story and then hope for the best.

Speeches

A speech will make news if it is made by some high-ranking company official and contains some newsworthy information on his company's sales and profit outlook, or expansion plans, or predictions of things to come. In other words, a speech is news if it contains news—not otherwise. On rare occasions, if the speaker takes a controversial stand on some business or political issue, it may rate coverage, but newpapers do not have time or space to print every routine public utterance of every top executive.

In servicing the business page, simply send a copy of the speech (in advance if possible) with a summary, to the business editor and cross your fingers. It might find its way into the news columns or it might be passed on to a reporter as background material.

Stock Tables

Expert statisticians—not reporters—prepare the tabulated stock quotation tables which appear in major

144

newspapers. They get their information directly from the stock exchanges and commodity markets, and the only material they need or will accept from publicity men are dividend reports.

Bonds

Like stocks, bonds can be purchased directly from the corporation or from the government, or they can be bought and sold through the nation's money markets or stock exchanges. A report of this trading is carried daily on the financial pages of larger newspapers, but the volume of trading is given in total dollar amounts rather than in the number of shares.

The bond reporter also reports new offerings by corporations and governments. His major sources of information are the stock exchanges and brokerage houses, but he also welcomes announcements of offerings from individual companies. Press releases on bond offerings are highly technical documents in themselves and must be prepared or supervised by qualified financial executives of the company. This is no job for amateurs.

The rules of accuracy and completeness must be strictly followed. A decimal point in the wrong place could have serious repercussions for the company.

NOTE: Coverage of industries includes industry-wide wrap-ups as well as news of individual companies. The reporter assigned to chemicals, for example, will from time to time bring his readers up to date on the sales, production and price outlook for the entire industry. He does this by surveying individual companies. This is an opportunity for the publicity man to get his company a mention by putting together accurate and meaningful information on his company's prospects and his bosses' opinions of the outlook for the industry as a whole.

Special Business Publications

The publicity man servicing business news is not confined to the business pages of the daily newspapers to tell his story. He can reach out to industrial journals and to unique publications like *The Wall Street Journal, Barron's,* and *The Journal of Commerce.*

Of the group, *The Wall Street Journal* is the most important publication from the publicity man's point of view. *The Journal of Commerce,* although similar in concept, does not offer the same broad range of business news, nor has it gained the readership and prestige of the WSJ. It deals primarily with commerce and deals with it in depth. Only by studying *The Journal of Commerce* can the publicity man decide whether his news fits into its editorial scheme of things.

Barron's, primarily a financial paper, deals with analyses of market trends, industry, and the like, and seldom uses publicity material.

The Wall Street Journal

Truly a national business paper by virtue of its four regional editions, *The Wall Street Journal* has jumped in circulation from about 65,000 readers in 1950 to more than 750,000 ten years later.

William F. Kerby, editorial director, explained in *Editor and Publisher* a little of the paper's editorial philosophy. Said Mr. Kerby:

"*The Wall Street Journal's* techniques of news handling have been evolutionary rather than revolutionary. The broadening concept of business has expanded our

146

field of reporting. While *The Journal* is written primarily for the business man and is an economic newspaper, a national business newspaper, many seemingly non-business stories actually have economic implications.

"Fires, rapes and scandals are out," he continued. "But all serious news is of interest to the business man. The whole field of serious news is our field. You can't get broader than that. All our news is national, although it may be local in origin. *The Journal* does not compete with any local paper. We would not cover a mayor's race in Philadelphia just because we have many readers there, but if the race should assume national implications, then we would run a story on it."

In servicing *The Wall Street Journal,* the publicity man will be as successful with the reporter as with the news editor and managing editor. There is no city editor here. Each reporter is responsible for a specific beat and is constantly in search of solid news in his area. Keep in mind *The Journal's* advice to new reporters on developing Page One lead stories:

1. Choose a subject of broad interest.
2. Reporting must be thorough and in depth.
3. Writing must be tightly packed and well organized around the central theme.

Reaction to sloppy releases is even more violent here than in most newspaper offices, for *The Journal* has a fetish about good writing and insists on good, clear, fact-packed stories. (One editor once suggested two facts to a line.)

In trying to break *The Wall Street Journal,* keep in mind that your material is competing for space with the output of one of the largest staffs of business editors and reporters in the country—approximately 120 writer-reporters and 50 editors—plus Associated Press, United Press International and Reuters.

This is a tough nut to crack, but it can be done if you really have a story to tell and take the pains to tell it well and present it interestingly and readably. Except for its basic emphasis on business news, submitting material to *The Wall Street Journal* is no different from submitting material to any other newspaper.

Trade Papers

The trade press is the bread-and-butter publicity medium for the commercial and industrial publicity man.

Banking, finance, chemicals, electronics, wholesaling, drugs and cosmetics, retailing, advertising, and management are only a few of the key areas represented by at least one newspaper or magazine. Some of these publications, though not generally considered trade magazines in the strictest sense, are geared to the interests of the entire business community. Others, like *Business Week, Forbes,* and *Fortune,* cater to a wider market of readers both in and out of business.

These publications provide the publicity man with a unique market for the kind of prestige publicity that is not often come by, not even on the business pages of the daily papers. Trade publications provide more than just an excellent medium for spreading company gospel about technical achievements or financial growth. They also offer the publicity man an outlet that can produce direct sales. In fact, the trade press is, perhaps, the only medium where your publicity effort can actually be measured in a dollar return.

New Products

This kind of dollar payoff is achieved through the trade magazines' varied and extensive "new products" sections. For this reason, new-product stories constitute more than thirty per cent of all publicity material received by trade magazine editors.

Product publicity has become a significant part of product promotion. Rubbing shoulders with other sales and advertising techniques, it is becoming increasingly important as a means of creating new product acceptance. Originally, it was relegated to the advertising department or the advertising agency and erroneously referred to as a "free ride" or free advertising. For years, this attitude cheated many firms of one of their most potent merchandising tools.

When public relations thinking and publicity techniques became more sophisticated, the product publicity assignment fell to specialists in that field. Nevertheless, although there are many top-grade publicity people doing an excellent job, this area of publicity handling still comes under attack by editors. The primary reason seems to be a throwback to the old days—lingering traces of the "advertising bait" approach. Publicity people, even some of the most astute, cannot seem to resist the temptation to apply pressure through the advertising department. It often works, but it does little to endear the publicity man or his company to the trade editors.

Edwin C. Mead, former editor of *Electrical Equipment*, prescribes this list of "Do's" for servicing product publicity to an industrial journal:

1. Be certain product is actually new or basically improved (not just new handle, fancy "package," or other minor change) .

149

2. Be sure product is available, on production basis, at the time release is mailed. If it is still in development or prototype stage, release should make this plain.

3. Provide brief, but *complete* description (include model or type number, or other exact product identification), giving basic operating principle (if applicable), *all* important specifications, and typical applications. If technical literature is available (and it should be—see 13 below), send along a copy.

4. Include at least one good-quality glossy photo or reproducible line drawing, if at all possible. Keep all wording, components, and other detail large enough so it will still be legible when illustration is reduced, and this may be as much as eighty-five per cent reduction on 8 x 10 photo.

5. Check your mailing lists at least once a year to be sure that your releases are being forwarded to the right person, as well as to *all* appropriate magazines.

6. Include *full* name and address of product manufacturer or other marketing organization. Also give name of person to whom reader inquiries should be directed.

7. Provide name and phone number of person and organization sending in the release, and from whom further information may be obtained by the editor.

8. Do a neat, legible job! All other things being equal, a carefully prepared story will be accepted before a sloppy one. Copy should be double-

spaced, on one side of the sheet only, and composed with short, unambiguous sentences.

9. Be precise! At least three different people should proofread all product releases before mailing. If the product is at all technical, one of these three people should be an engineer or other trained person who can spot technical errors or misleading statements.

10. Explain highly specialized terms that may not be commonly understood by engineers, executives, and other readers not directly connected with the product manufacturer's field. Unfortunately, even editors can't know everything about everything.

11. Put facts in order of relative importance. Cover major features in opening paragraphs, minor attributes at the end of the release.

12. Provide a "sum-up" announcement along with technical releases that require more than two pages of exposition.

13. When release is mailed, have literature ready to send to readers who want more data on product.

14. Keep a file of copies of magazines to which you send releases. This will help you prepare publicity by showing you *how* each magazine handles product announcements, and *what kind* of products they accept for publication.

15. Consider the possibility of mailing "case history" stories. They offer a means of providing "news" (in the form of new applications) about a product that may not itself be new.

16. Send out condensed catalog or data sheet—once every year or two—covering all your company's products. This material is worthwhile for editors'

files and may be useful in subsequent "buyer's guide" as well as for answering readers' "where-can-I-buy-it" requests.

A common error made by publicity men dealing with the trade press is the sending of covering letters to accompany a release. Industrial editors without exception object to this practice.

Gordon H. Bixler of *Chemical and Engineering News* speaks for all editors when he says:

"My chief complaint about publicity men is their practice of putting a covering letter on top of a release, a letter that goes on a great length about what a great company our client is and how much we think your readers will want to know about this most significant development they have come up with—without saying what the development is!

"The development is described in the attached release, to be sure, but you have to wade through a long letter to find out what gives. Most releases should speak for themselves. I doubt that many editors are impressed with a selling job in a covering letter. If the editor doesn't know companies and products without such letters, he has no business being an editor."

John H. Van Deventer of *Purchasing Magazine,* says flatly, "Do away with an introductory letter: 'Good morning, dear editor. We are proud to be able to submit our release to your fine publications ... etc. .... etc. .... etc.' "

The publicist who carefully analyzes the trade market should produce solid coverage for his client or his company. Although a few of these publications will accept almost anything to fill space, most of them insist on material that fits their format. The mass-produced release, the release that is not designed expressly for this market, will miss the mark in many publications or else will be boiled down into a small space.

Keep in mind that this also is an area ripe for solid feature coverage. By digging out the unusual or the offbeat, and by presenting in the style of the publication you want to reach, you can make an impressive showing.

While some trade and industrial publications are independently published, others are part of major publishing empires, as is the case with McGraw-Hill Publishing Company, Inc., and Fairchild Publications, Inc.

Fairchild Publications

Fairchild publishes three business dailies: *Women's Wear Daily, Daily News Record,* and *Home Furnishings Daily;* five weeklies: *Drug News Weekly, Footwear News, Supermarket News, Electronic News,* and *Metalworking News;* and a semi-monthly magazine, *Men's Wear Magazine.*

Women's Wear stands alone in prestige in the retail and soft goods fields and practices rigid editorial standards not even to be found on many general daily newspapers.

The accent at Fairchild is on news, and the publications pride themselves on collecting news without resorting to outside sources. That is, they get their news through their reporting staffs working directly with the news source, not with public relations or publicity men.

Stephen S. Marks, Editor of the *Daily News Record,* expresses the Fairchild point of view when he says:

"We insist upon our reporters getting intimate with their respective beats, by constant calling upon the people making news."

He added, "We just don't like PR people. Our reporters are encouraged to get the news first, ahead of the PR people who are generally slow, angle their releases, which often are incomplete and full of advertising."

For this reason, the Fairchild publications depend upon a network of thirty-seven news bureaus here and abroad. The bureaus are manned by 139 writers and reporters, and in addition there are approximately 388 stringers scattered through 353 cities in this country and fifty abroad.

Fairchild reporters are noted for digging, diligence and tenacity. One retail public relations director says he puts all mail and other correspondence out of sight when one of the Fairchild men is due to arrive.

"Nothing is off the record with them," he says, "so you hide anything you don't want to see in the newspaper."

Despite Fairchild's announced indifference to publicity people, a publicity man with real news and no puff stands a good chance for coverage in their publications. Here again the ground rules for working with the working press apply.

McGraw-Hill Publications

McGraw-Hill publishes some thirty weekly, monthly, and bi-monthly magazines, among them *Business Week, Chemical Week, Electrical World, Electronics, Purchasing Week, Coal Age, Control Engineering, Factory, National Petroleum News, Textile World*. Other publications delve into the fields of product engineering, construction work, food engineering, machinist-metalworking, architecture.

Frances Oliver, News Manager for the McGraw-Hill publications, says that working with the industrial press does not differ too greatly from working with the general daily press except for one factor:

"Most of our editors agree," she says, "that the one important difference is the necessity for knowing the publication to which you are sending your releases.

"This is also important with the general press, but not to the same extent. Our publications are chiefly business, technical, and scientific, and a press agent who did not understand the specific area they cover would have virtually no chance of hitting the right publication with the right release. In most cases, the story must be tailor-made for the publication, and the smartest press agents are the ones who take the trouble to know the magazine before they try to write for it.

"The editor wants n e w s—in his field. He wants it complete and on time, and above all, he wants it reliable. Our editors—like editors everywhere—want information that they know their readers will be interested in, and when you give them that, you can be virtually sure of acceptance. They want specific facts in the specific areas for which their publications are produced."

Unlike many trade or industrial publishers, McGraw-Hill goes to great lengths to help the publicity person to know the magazine. Printed booklets and mimeographed forms describing the editorial concept of each publication are available upon request.

Typical is the information found in the booklet, "Tips on Writing for FACTORY."

"Urgent and timely, that's the way your article must sound to win and hold the attention of a reader. FACTORY's readers are busy men. Standard, routine good practice alone is not enough to win and hold them. They want to know, quickly and clearly, what's new, what's unusual, what's different and rewarding about your subject.

"Generally articles that cut a wide swath across readers' interests are the best kind for FACTORY readers. Try to keep in mind the readers you're writing for. Try to imagine what they want to know and how the things you're writing about will affect them and their jobs.

"And, by the way, don't overlook time and place in your article: Name and location of company and plant you're writing about, and time that's significant for the story you tell."

In the booklet, "How To Write For PRODUCT ENGINEERING," the McGraw-Hill attitude toward press releases is outlined:

"We welcome press releases and news announcements from manufacturing companies and their public relations or advertising departments or agencies. But the releases must be about really new or unique products, materials or equipment. As a general practice, we do not publish announcements of personnel changes and promotions, nor announcements or reports of local or regional professional meetings.

"When we use a press release, we rewrite it (and often seek more information from the source) to make it fit the needs and interests of our readers."

9

WORKING WITH
THE WOMAN'S PAGE

THE WOMAN'S PAGE of any newspaper has one primary
function: To satisfy the interests of its women readers.
Since women today are interested in everything and
anything, a well-edited Woman's Page will offer a little
bit of everything and anything.

Not too long ago, the principal emphasis was on
society news, the assumption being that every woman who
picked up the paper would be charmed and enchanted by
accounts of the goings-on among the community's so-
called elite. The society page and the woman's page were
one and the same.

Today, the smart woman's page editor knows that her
readers are much more likely to be charmed and enchanted by accounts of their own goings-on or the goings-
on of their neighbors. As a consequence, on many newspapers the woman's page and the society page are now
two separate departments.

Today's woman's pages reflect modern woman's great
diversity of interests and are likely to feature in adjoining
columns a lively interview with the First Lady, an article
on how to mix paints, and an account of last night's fund-

raising dinner dance on behalf of the local Community Chest.

Generally speaking, the news and features appearing on this page fall into specific areas of interest, and an editor or reporter is usually assigned to handle each of the following:

1. Fashion
2. Food
3. Beauty
4. Home furnishings
5. Community events
6. Child care and teen news
7. Advice and counseling
8. Society news
9. Church news

On smaller papers, of course, one staff member may double on two or more categories. On others, as we have noted, the society news and the church news may be given separate pages.

Because of the wide range of interests represented, the woman's page of a newspaper offers the publicity person a frequent and fruitful outlet for his material. With one or two possible exceptions (such as child care and counseling features) all these interest areas are open to stories from the outside. Moreover, they are open to stories with a frankly commercial flavor—something that is not true of the general news columns of the paper.

This does not mean, however, that when you are dealing in fashion, food, beauty, et al., that you can throw away the rule book of journalism. In this respect, the woman's page editor is no different from any other editor: She wants—and prints—news.

This may be the latest word on Paris fashions, the

election of a new Parent-Teacher Association president, or the appearance on the market of a new kind of dishwasher. All of these stories are clearly slanted to the interests of women, but they also have news value.

Oddly enough, the sympathetic eye and ear of the woman's page editor seem to receive the most abuse from the very publicity people whose special interest stories are grist to the woman's page mill. Within an eight-hour period, a woman's page editor will receive more worthless press releases, more long-winded and pointless telephone calls, and more interruptions and personal intrusions than any other departmental editor on the paper.

Eleanor Parrish, Woman's Editor for *The News Journal* of Wilmington, Del., has run out of patience on this score.

"I don't see," she says, "how I can face all day long the stupid, inane and inaccurate material some (publicity people) send me." She described some of the press releases that reach her as "outrageous samples of ruinously multilithed pap!"

One explanation for such a record of abuse is that so many non-professionals are active in this area of publicity and press relations. Women's clubs, PTAs, fraternal organizations, small retail shops, trade groups and professional organizations seldom can afford a full-time publicity expert. Moreover, in these groups, the publicity job changes hands from year to year, and no one stays at it long enough to profit by the experience.

Marie Anderson, Woman's Editor of *The Miami* (Fla.) *Herald*, lists this practice as her favorite complaint.

"I know the individual clubs like to pass the jobs around among the members," she says, "but whenever they get a good publicity chairman, I encourage them to keep her for more than one year. Gathering news is a talent, and through the years we have had some very good amateur reporters' aides in club publicity chairmen.

"They don't know how to do it when they take the job, however, and just as they're learning, the year is up and we start all over."

Miss Anderson added: "If the club group is large—a council or federation—I suggest a professional publicity person. And the biggest part of his job will be getting all members to channel information through him."

Pride and Prejudice

It is not the amateurs alone who assault the ear and insult the intelligence of the woman's page staff. The professional publicist is often just as guilty, and with less excuse.

Although most woman's pages offer essentially the same kind of news and feature material, the over-all format varies from paper to paper because each editor prides herself on the individuality and style of her page. Yet professional publicists (as well as amateurs) consistently ignore the personality of the page when they send off their releases. (This, incidentally, is a complaint heard in all other departments of the newspaper.)

"I'm constantly amazed," said one recipient of these missent missiles, "at how many topflight public relations men apparently don't take the trouble to read the newspaper they are trying to interest in printing their material.

"If they studied the content of the newspaper, they would know, for instance, that a cheesecake picture of a bikini-clad model holding an air hammer will not be used on the traditionally conservative business page of the average newspaper. Nor would the story of a company merger make any sense on the woman's page. Yet every mail brings a batch of this sort of misdirected material."

And Miss Anderson of *The Miami Herald* adds:

"I'd suggest the professional public relations man read some woman's pages before he comes in with story ideas.

"We stopped running long lists of area chairmen years ago. And my idea of a bathing fashion story isn't a plane junket to Nassau and back for the members of the Northwest South Woman's Club. Who besides the ladies who took the trip cares, and what is new in the swimsuits?"

Recipe for Woman's Page

Constance Woodworth, Woman's Page Editor of *The New York Journal-American,* outlines the philosophy of her department this way:

"We edit our pages not for the ladies who write our stories; not for the ladies who are the source of our stories; and we try not to edit them for the gruff voices of the advertising department. We edit our pages consistently and without deviation for the reader who pays the dime."

If you are a publicist whose client is also an advertiser with the newspaper, think twice—and once again—before you exert pressure upon the woman's page editor through the advertising department. As we have said before, and probably will say again, nothing will guarantee you the lasting antagonism of a newspaper editor more surely than outside pressure of this sort.

As Miss Woodworth points out:

"I feel there is no reason why a woman's department should be considered a coop for frustrated, daffy females or be regarded as a problem child or a necessary evil to appease advertisers. Woman's pages all over the country have come down from their attics and into the editorial family."

Although the bulk of the material appearing in the woman's pages may seem frivolous compared to the dramatic, earth-shaking contents of Pages One, Two or Three, the compiling of the woman's page is a serious business, requiring the dedication and talents of many highly-trained newspaper professionals.

Traditionally, specialized departments such as the woman's page handle the page in magazine fashion — that is, although the content is always timely, it is not necessarily late-breaking news. Rather, it is of a nature that generally can sustain its interest throughout all editions.

(Most daily newspapers print several editions of one day's paper, and some large dailies have as many as five or six editions. As fast-breaking news develops throughout the day it is included in the next edition, keeping the news as fresh and timely as possible.)

On some newspapers, the woman's page editor now competes with the pages of the city side by not "freezing" her page for the run of the paper, and by opening it between editions if timely news comes in.

"The thing that will hold the most interest for the most women on any given day is the thing we play," says *The Journal-American's* Editor Woodworth. "If Page One must lure its readers by shouting, the woman's page must do it with a wink, or a flirtatious smile, or the saucy swirl of a skirt."

Miss Woodworth has compiled a list of Do's and Don'ts for the publicity beginner who is trying to break into the woman's page of *The Journal-American* in New York. We think it is good advice for amateurs and professionals dealing with the woman's page of any newspaper, anywhere.

1. *Do* put more effort into your writing. The amount of bad phrasing, poor English and even misspelling is appalling.
2. *Do* be more constructive. Work with us, not on an island of your own. After all, you are a liaison between your product (or organization or company) and the newspaper, and sometimes, you are the only one we can turn to for information and help.
3. *Do* take pride in your work. It is a fine field, a necessary field, and from one newspaperwoman's viewpoint, an important part of making a better paper.
4. *Don't* make your crises ours by creating a deadline. We have our own problems. (Note: This department, like all others, has a fixed schedule of deadlines. Learn it.)
5. *Don't* turn out a third-rate job by guessing on your subject. Know it thoroughly and stick to it.
6. *Don't* send a snippy letter saying you've sent releases on your clients with no results, and you see no reason why you should be slighted.
7. *Don't* walk into an editor's office with a chip on your shoulder or a know-it-all attitude. And don't come in as though you were spending the afternoon. Get down to business. Get it over with. Then depart.

The Editor Wants to Know

There is certain basic information you must always communicate to a newspaper, no matter which department you are dealing with, and the techniques involved are taken up in detail in Chapter 5, "The Press Release."

The woman's page, however, is a specialized "market." Many details that would not be acceptable to other sections of the paper—that would, in fact, be frowned upon —are perfectly legitimate, even necessary on the woman's page.

Here is a run-down on some of the stories a woman's page will use and how you can present them.

Fashion

The woman's page editor is always looking for seasonal fashion features (Thanksgiving, Christmas, Spring, Back-to-School) and for features on specific articles of apparel or accessories. Study the page in which you are trying to place your publicity and try to anticipate the editor's needs.

The professional publicist sending press releases to the woman's page should include this information in a release on fashion items: price, sizes, style numbers, colors, unique features, name of designer, name of manufacturer, stores where it is available.

The amateur, the publicity chairman for the club's fashion show, will find that the woman's page editor is far more interested in a show that centers around a particular theme or kind of apparel (hats, for instance, or shoes, suits, lounge wear, coats, furs) than she is in the usual collection of miscellaneous clothing donated by a local department store.

Persuade your club to produce this kind of a show, and then alert the woman's page editor well in advance. Do this with a press release, and follow through later with other releases (see Chapter 5.) See Chapter 7 for instructions on how to accommodate the reporter and photographer who have been assigned to cover the show.

Food

The recipe has been a fixture on women's pages for decades and it has not lost its place to the new features which have come along in recent years. Food, if anything, is more important to the housewife today than ever before. She has learned the importance of preparing nutritious, non-fattening meals for her family, and she is hard put to keep up with the innovations in frozen foods and ready mixes.

Newspapers, accordingly, are devoting more space to food news than ever before. Some papers run weekly food pages or sections. Almost all of them give plenty of space regularly to recipes, pictures and features. Food editors are so numerous that there are literally hundreds in attendance at the food editors' conventions each year.

The professional trying to place food product publicity will focus her attention on the food pages. These usually run on the days when heavy grocery advertising appears in the paper.

Some papers will not use a brand name of a product in a story, but will use stories showing how a particular product can be used. This is a risk you'll have to take. If they delete "Yummy Canned Peaches" from your copy, you'll just have to be content with the fact they are giving the housewife the idea to buy peaches, and hope she'll pick Yummy's when she gets to the store.

Here again it pays to anticipate the needs of the editor. A food editor will be looking for good and novel features for Thanksgiving, Christmas, Easter, the Jewish High Holy Days and other holidays. Warm weather menus and diet suggestions are always welcome, too. If you represent certain fruits or vegetables, get your stories or recipes to her so that they can run when they're in season.

Sharp, mouth-watering pictures are always in demand, but don't put the can of Yummy peaches in the foreground. Pictures of holiday or party table settings are always appreciated, too.

Products

In mailing out releases for product publicity, include the following information: Prices, what it does, how it works, colors, unique features, name of manufacturer, stores where it is available, brand names, model number.

Here again, you run the risk of having the brand name deleted from your copy. One thing about a marvelous new potato peeler, however—the woman's page editor who deletes the brand name will get plenty of phone calls the next day, and your client will get some publicity after all.

Home Furnishings

Editors are constantly looking for news of style trends in home furnishings and for tips on remodeling, redecorating and maintaining the home. If you represent any home furnishings manufacturer, your press releases will be welcomed by the woman's department.

Don't bear down too hard on the commercial, however, or your entire release may hit the wastebasket. Your copy should be designed to whet the housewife's interest in buying a new bedroom set or remodeling the bathroom. You can best do this by suggesting decorating ideas instead of hammering away at the theme that your company makes dandy shower curtains. She probably already has perfectly good shower curtains. What she needs is an incentive to throw them away and buy new ones that will go with the new decorating scheme YOU have suggested.

Even though all the information may not be printed, you must include these facts in your home furnishings release: price, colors, sizes, unique features, name of manufacturer, stores where it is available, brand names.

Beauty

Under this general heading come many topics of interest to women: hair styles, grooming, make-up, figure control. Publicists for everything from hairpins to toe rings should be able to fit their products into this category of woman's page news if they use a little imagination.

Offer the editor news of the latest styles of make-up—and casually mention your product after you are into the body of the story. Show how the product can be used in unusual ways. Give out with helpful hints—when to wear eye shadow, how to heal chapped lips, how to pick a becoming hair style, how to lose two inches off the waistline.

Note: Whenever you are naming the retail outlet for a product, or a dress or draperies, be certain that you have first cleared all your facts with either the individual buyer or the store's public relations representative. Often the store no longer carries the item, or it may have sold out. Possibly the store never stocked the item in the first place; maybe it has changed the price.

167

Checking out these details will avert headaches all around—for the client, the store, the editor and you.

Teens

In recent years, the woman's page has begun to cover the interests of teen-agers. Many woman's departments have editors who prepare a weekly page of news and features exclusively for the younger generation. Fashions, records, amusements, snacks, spectator sports, etiquette and advice to the love-lorn are all welcome here.

Publicists can help the editor keep up with the fads in dress and can weave good features around these fads. Be certain, before you send off your press release, that your story has a built-in interest for teen-agers. Otherwise, save it for some other department.

Churches

There is no hard and fast rule about where church news appears in the daily newspapers. Sometimes it appears in the general news columns, occasionally on the woman's pages, and often on the "church page."

Some papers use sermon topics and general church news such as building plans, appointment of a new pastor, and other such items in the general news columns of the papers. The woman's pages then get the news of a social nature—bazaars, ladies' aid meetings, rallies and rummage sales.

The publicity chairman will do well to check the newspaper for information of how the various stories should be submitted and then submit material accordingly. (See Chapter 5, "The Press Release.")

Getting Along in Society

If the newspapers you deal with handle society news separately from the woman's page, a phone call to the papers will produce the name of the proper editor. In any case, the news that is considered "society," and the way in which it is handled, do not differ greatly from paper to paper. The greatest variation will be a matter of perspective—an engagement announcement that may not rate a line in *The New York Times* or *The Chicago Tribune* will get much more play in the hometown daily or weekly.

Society news generally is concerned with the activities of the community's socially prominent citizens as they are born, "come out," become engaged, get married, and take part in fund-raising and charitable activities.

(If these same socially prominent citizens should become divorced or turn up murdered, they no longer would belong on the society page.)

This is one part of the paper where the old maxim, "Names make news," applies in force. A report on the fashion show benefiting the hospital drive, for instance, may devote priceless inches to long lists of names of the club women active on various committees.

In some papers, you will find a "Society Column," a column which passes on "gossip" about society people and society-sponsored affairs. Such a column gives an editor more flexibility than do the news columns, and items that do not necessarily deserve special coverage or a straight story often find a happy berth in this column.

The bulk of society news, however, usually deals with the matrimonial activities of a community's socially prominent, and for this reason, it is important to know how to handle both an engagement announcement and a

169

wedding story. You may one day have to send such releases to newspapers on behalf of an organization, a client —or yourself.

Just whose engagement or which wedding qualifies for space on the local society page will vary from paper to paper and from community to community. Naturally, the hometown weekly has a lot more space and latitude for this kind of news than the nearby small city daily. And the small city daily will have requirements considerably different from those of the metropolitan dailies in large cities.

But regardless of these highly individual aspects of the society page, certain information is vital and unvarying.

The Engagement Announcement

Announcement of an engagement is usually made by the girl's parents. The release should include the following information:

1. Full name of the girl
2. Full name of the boy
3. Places of residence of each
4. Names of girl's parents
5. Names of boy's parents
6. Places of residence of both sets of parents
7. Parents' professional or business affiliations and positions
8. Education background of the girl and place of employment, if any. Current activity in any case
9. Education background of the young man and his professional affiliation
10. Community affairs activities of all involved—par-

ents and couple—assuming these activities warrant mention

11. Projected date for wedding (not a must)

A typical engagement release would be written something like this:

"Mr. and Mrs. A. B. Dee of Bell Harbor have announced the engagement of their daughter, Miss Cynthia Sheila Dee, to John Jones Jr., son of Mr. and Mrs. John Jones of Bronxville, New York, and Miami, Fla.

"The bride-to-be is an alumna of Smith Junior College and earned a Bachelor of Arts degree at the University of Maryland.

"Mr. Jones is an alumnus of New York University and is employed as an assistant vice president of the XYZ Company. Mr. Jones's father is chairman of the board of the XYZ Company and a director of the First National Bank of Bronxville.

"Mr. Dee is a former Vice President of the ABC Metals Company and is currently chairman of the Bell Harbor Community Chest Campaign."

The wedding story contains the same information as the engagement announcement, with these additions:

12. Date of wedding
13. Place and time of ceremony
14. Officiating pastor
15. Name of best man and ushers
16. Name of maid or matron of honor and of bridesmaids
17. Description of the bride's gown
18. If it's really a big wedding, describe the bride's attendants' gowns, and name ring bearer, flower girl, etc.

19. Description of gowns of bride's mother and bride-groom's mother
20. Time and place of reception or wedding breakfast
21. Number of guests in attendance
22. Honeymoon destination (if known)
23. The residence of the newlyweds

Your own good judgment will have to determine how much of the details from 18-21 you will include, if any.

In any event, don't be carried away by the romance of the occasion. Leave the "lovely," "charming," "beautiful," and "exquisite," out of the story. Save them for the bride and her family on the receiving line, and spare the society editor.

(Note: Some newspapers provide wedding and engagement announcement forms for readers to fill out and send in. Others like *The New York Times* and *The New York Herald Tribune* merely advise their callers to read the paper and follow the format.)

Summary

Servicing the woman's page with publicity is no different from servicing any other section of the newspaper. The invitation for press coverage, the editorial approach, the preparation of press releases and accommodation of the press at special events should be handled exactly as outlined in Chapters 5 and 7, respectively. The only difference will be in the nature of the story or news involved.

Remember that competition for space in the woman's page is extremely keen and that your story will be just one of hundreds being considered. It will have to be well-prepared and well-presented to command attention.

Ideally, of course, you would approach the newspaper

Evening • $\mathfrak{Newark}$ $\mathfrak{News}$ • **Sunday**

Bride's name _____

Bride's parents and residence and phone no. _____

_____

_____

Bridegroom's name _____

Bridegroom's parents and residence and phone no. _____

_____

_____

Date and hour of wedding _____

Place of wedding _____

Place of reception _____

Clergyman, of what church _____

(List attendants' relationship to couple, if any)

Maid and matron of honor _____

_____

Bridesmaids (if married, give husband's first name) _____

_____

_____

Flower girl _____

Ring bearer _____

Best man _____

Ushers _____

College graduated from or attended by bride and bridegroom _____

_____

Business affiliations _____

_____

SAMPLE WEDDING ANNOUNCEMENT FORM

only when you have a solid, legitimate story. Before you send in your story, ask yourself this question:

"Honestly, is this story of real interest to all women readers? Does it really belong in the papers?"

If you can answer "yes," be sure you have all the facts, write your story in clear and uncomplicated language—and send it along.

10

WORKING WITH
SPECIALIZED DEPARTMENTS

EVERY NEWSPAPER features a number of specialized departments devoted to a limited-interest subject that commands a numerically substantial group of readers. The woman's page represents such a reader group. So does the business and financial page. Because of their wide-ranging interests, these two departments offer a fertile, though specialized, field for the publicist or publicity chairman with a story to tell. For this reason, we have devoted two full chapters to these departments. (See Chapter 9, "Working With the Woman's Page," and Chapter 8, "Working With the Business Page.")

There are a number of interest areas, however, whose range is so limited that except for the highly-specialized publicity man, they do not provide easy berths for most publicity stories. (Some of these are not departments at all, but "beats," which are usually handled off the city desk. The man or woman assigned is nonetheless an "editor" with the responsibility for covering an entire field such as science, medicine, education, labor. The stories covered by these reporters, rather than being relegated on one particular page, may crop up anywhere from Page One to the obituary columns.)

175

Here is a list of some of the special interests usually represented in most newspapers:

Sports
Entertainment
Travel
Gardening
Real Estate
Obituaries
Schools
Books and Art

Not all these subjects rate a full page or section in all newspapers. Some may be only columns, but on special occasions they may be expanded into full pages or sections —such as a gardening section in the Spring or a boating section in the Summer.

In some papers, the specialized department is an arm of advertising, and its sole purpose is to bolster advertising revenues. The travel section is a good example. On some newspapers, the non-advertiser is anathema to the travel editor who is interested only in giving space to his advertisers. Sometimes the editor and advertising space salesman are the same person, an impregnable bastion for the publicity man whose client does not advertise.

For the special-interest publicist or the publicity chairman who might represent such a group, here is an analysis of each specialized department and of the chances for publicity stories in each.

Sports

Sports enjoy unprecedented prestige in America today. Many readers turn to the sports page before they scan the front page headlines of their favorite newspaper

—unless, of course, the front page features an account of some major sporting event such as a World Series, heavyweight championship bout or the Kentucky Derby.

Although sports sections have been trimmed in space in recent years to offset increased newsprint and production costs, their staffs are as large as or larger than those of most other specialized departments. This is in great part due to the increased popularity of heretofore limited-interest sports such as boating, golf, or bowling and to the increased numbers of new leagues and new teams in the traditionally popular sports. Most large newspapers still assign reporters to accompany baseball and football teams and turn out full crews of reporters and photographers to cover all angles of a major sports event.

When you consider the wide range of events crowded into the sports pages every day, you can understand why these pages are generally not open to publicity stories. You seldom find a non-sports item on this page, and unles you are doing a publicity job for a sports personality, team or league, you will find an unsympathetic customer in the sports editor. Even seemingly appropriate clients such as sports goods manufacturers or stores or company sports events find it tough sledding, especially on larger papers.

There are occasions when the non-sports publicity man can break the ice. This usually is done through the sports columnist whose range of subject matter is somewhat more flexible. A new book on baseball for boys or the results of a club's bowling championship playoffs would stand a chance here.

(There is a matter of perspective always to be kept in mind. We refer primarily to major newspapers of large circulations. Newspaper editors in small towns let down the bars in this area out of deference to community interests. Stories such as local bowling tournaments, company baseball competitions and the like will get plenty of coverage. Don't however, sell the small newspapers short. Even here, your publicity story must have a legitimate sports angle to justify space on the page.)

In the course of one day, a sports editor will have to juggle the following sports topics, and your publicity story will have to fit into one of these classifications if it is to stand a chance.

Football
Baseball
Basketball
Bowling
Boxing and wrestling
Hockey
Hunting and fishing
Horse racing
Track and field
Golf
Tennis
Boating
Auto racing
Ice skating — roller skating

Depending upon the season, each of the above subjects is covered in depth. The sports editor is interested in background stories on players, coaches and management, and in profiles on individual stars and their families. Sports news covers training sessions and new player acquisitions, scores and records and financial data such as gate receipts, salaries and prize money. As in other sections, the editor is the boss. If you have a story to tell, tell it to the editor in the manner prescribed in Chapters 4 and 5. The subjects may differ but publicity techniques remain the same.

Entertainment

There's no business like show business for the publicity man who is servicing entertainment accounts and/or individuals who want to establish reputations identifying them with show business. The entertainment page is one area where personal contacts are essential, and the better the contacts, the better the coverage.

Generally speaking, the subjects covered by the entertainment department tend to remain highly specialized; the movie writer concerns himself with movies and movie personalities, the music critic stays within his own sphere of knowledge, the drama critic sticks to the theater, and so forth.. What opens the department to the press agent are the newspapers' numerous columnists.

Working With the Columnist

The "about town" or "gossip" columnist is the mainstay of many a newspaper and often the mainstay of many a theatrical publicity man.

Charles McHarry, columnist for *The New York Daily News,* quite frankly announced his dependence upon press agents when his "On The Town" became a daily feature of the paper:

"We will rely to a great extent on press agents," said McHarry, "a hard-working pack without whom the 600 words, five days a week, would be killing. I suppose there are some columnists who can do the job without publicity men, but I wouldn't even try."

It is here that personal contact takes on its real meaning, and it is here that the publicity man finds his best opportunity to "plug" a wide range of subjects.

179

(These columns should not be confused with the other columns of comment which appear in the daily papers. Columns dealing with everything from world and government affairs to just plain humor are "personal journalism" at its best. They reflect the personality and thinking of the writer, seldom the special interests of the publicity man.)

Many publiciity men specialize in the area of entertainment column publicity exclusively, and because the "whom you know" is usually as important as the "what you know," they go to great lengths to cultivate friendships with columnists. According to those who've done it, the best way to do this is to keep the columnist supplied with a typewriter full of gossipy items.

If you are to succeed with a columnist, you must provide him with reliable information. Much of what he uses are "blind items," stories that do not mention names but leave the reader with strong suspicions, rumors that need not always be substantiated in print, tips on coming events. He must have a great deal of confidence in his publicity sources. For this reason, and unlike other newspapermen, the columnist works happily hand-in-hand with the publicity man.

Earl Wilson, one of the most respected syndicated columnists in the field, cheerfully makes this point:

"Some of my best friends are press agents. In fact, practically all my best friends are press agents. I like the kind of publicity man whom I can call up and say, 'Jack, I'd like to know the lowdown on this particular situation,' and I like to have the kind of relationship with this person where he will tell me even though it might be to the detriment of his client.

"He knows that in the future he's going to be dealing

with me about other clients, and, therefore, he'll tell me the truth."

This is the heart of the columnist-publicity man relationship. The publicity man must perform two functions if he wants to stay in business. In order to earn his "plug," he must first provide the columnist with real material, even if it is not publicity for his client. If he can produce a steady flow of this kind of information (providing it is accurate and exclusive), the columnist will then find room for the publicity items.

For this reason, in one week's columns a columnist may mention a great number of unrelated subjects such as real estate projects, dance studios, restaurants, politicians, country resorts, obscure entertainers, beauty parlors and soft drinks (all plugs), skillfully blended with items about the rich, the famous and the interesting (the real meat of the columnist).

In dealing with the entertainment page editor or any of his by-line writers, the usual press release or announcement will do.

In addition, this section is usually interested in good pictures and sound feature ideas. If the publicity man represents an up-and-coming entertainer with an unusual background, or a really different product or fad exclusive to show people, the editor will probably be interested.

Otherwise, stay away from this section unless you have a strong, heavily-accented entertainment story. The appearance of a celebrity at a club luncheon will not rate mention on this page (although it might do very well on the woman's page). And the story about an amateur theatrical will get nowhere here—unless you are dealing with a relatively small newspaper.

In smaller communities and on smaller newspapers,

the amateur theatrical or civic theater is given considerable community and editorial support. In the home-town weekly, a senior class play rates as much attention as the opening of a new Noel Coward production on Broadway.

Incidentally, pictures are a boon to small papers, but most weeklies are not set up to make engravings. It might pay you to try to arrange with a photoengraver (or a nearby daily) to make the plates for you to send to the weeklies. If there are a lot of weeklies to be serviced, you might go a step further and have mats made. They will be welcomed.

On larger newspapers high school theatricals may be covered on the school page or teen page or whatever provision the paper makes for taking note of the activities of the younger generation. But the local "civic theater," in most instances, will rate straight news coverage. This is because it is usually considered an important cultural asset. Even a commerical touring stock company will get press attention just because it's nice to have live theater in town.

In most cases, the publicity man for the civic theater group is a member who is also working as a stage hand or set designer or prompter. Caught up in the fever of the production, he or she will often forget until the last minute that the newspaper ought to be alerted to the fact that a show is forthcoming.

On the other hand, some civic groups go to the other extreme. They assume they've "got it made" where press coverage is concerned, and they take the newspaper for granted, expecting it to do all the work, take all the pictures and dream up all the features. This is a serious mistake. The critic or reviewer on the smaller newspaper usually writes all the other theater news and in addition

182

has half a dozen other miscellaneous assignments, plus a regular beat to cover.

The amateur publicist for the local theater group should follow the advice in Chapters 5 and 6 concerning press releases and pictures and service the newspaper as professionally as though his living depended on it.

Travel and Resorts

Most newspapers feature a travel and resort section at least once a week. On some papers, as we indicated earlier, this page or section exists as much for the advertisers' benefit as for the readers', since only advertisers get "news" coverage.

The travel page is the Number One target for any publicity man representing resorts, transportation companies, chambers of commerce or tourist boards; but many publicity people who represent areas of interest outside travel and resort groups have been able to use the travel page effectively.

Stories about natural wonders (Niagara Falls, the Grand Canyon), man-made wonders (Disneyland and Freedomland), camping sites and trails, camping equipment and experiences, summer sports, special events such as state festivals, music festivals and rodeos, may all appear on the travel page. A movie company may premiere a movie at a resort, and thus garner "bonus" publicity for the film on the travel page. (This kind of tie-in might also open the entertainment page to the resort.)

For the publicity man, the advertiser-controlled travel page is a source of mixed emotions, depending usually upon the size of his clients' advertising budgets.

To the travel writer and editor, however, this condition is viewed with a great deal of concern. It is also becoming a matter of concern to other, non-newspaper groups with a vested interest in the dissemination of travel news.

Robert Nelson of the Virginia Travel Council stressed this point at a meeting of the Society of American Travel Writers:

"We must sell the newspapers on the fact that the blurb is no more, that travel does create news, and it's news with more sales penetration with the reader than most other news. We must sell the newspapers on a complete divorce between the advertising and the news departments as it relates to travel. We must sell the editor on the fact that newspapers have a responsibility to the public for the sound, comprehensive development of travel facilities."

The Society of American Travel Writers ethical code might give the publicity man concerned with this area a clue to the travel writer's point of view.

1. The travel writer's primary obligation is to serve his readers with truthful, complete and helpful detailed reports on travel destination, facilities and services.

2. He must at all times seek to broaden his reader's vacation horizon in every possible way by providing them with fresh, newsworthy information on all aspects of pleasure travel.

3. Recognizing the increasingly important role of travel in fostering international friendship and understanding, the travel writer will, whenever possible, seek to acquaint his readers with the many possibilities for people-to-people contacts, the pursuit of special interest projects and other aspects of travel far more rewarding than mere sightseeing.

4. The travel writer should serve as a travel critic and be as ready to praise as to condemn. As the representative of his readers, he will protest or otherwise draw attention to inadequacies of service, comfort or cleanliness, while at the same time attempting to help the travel purveyor by offering constructive suggestions for correcting these deficiencies.

5. No travel writer should allow himself to be persuaded to write about a vacation destination he has not visited or a facility or service he has not experienced unless personal knowledge of his informant convinces him the details are true and complete.

6. The travel writer cannot be obligated to publicize an operation. His expressed reactions and opinions must be his own.

7. The travel writer should regard all group press trips in which he participates as working trips during which he will make every effort to obtain and to report with objectivity travel news items of interest to his readers.

This last item, the "group press trip," is known usually as a junket, and it has long been a popular tool of the travel and resort publicity man. But at this writing, the junket was being junked. More and more editors look on it as a form of "payola"—which is to be avoided like the plague,—and is considered too time consuming and unproductive to be worthwhile.

On the advertiser-controlled travel page, a routine press release or a phone call is enough to get the story across to the travel editor (providing, of course, your client is an advertiser).

On this kind of travel page, almost any publicity will go. The usual picture of a pretty gal standing poolside is sure fire, as is a photo of the resort owner stiffly shaking hands with some new arrival.

Some advertisers, jaded with the "paid" publicity they receive, have begun pressing their publicity men for coverage in other parts of the paper such as gossip columns or the news pages. Most news editors and columnists have managed to resist this pressure so far, since this kind of stuff is adequately covered on the travel page.

In newspapers where the travel page is a legitimate member of the editorial family, the best way to reach the editor is through the standard press release.

As in any other area of publicity handling, the best way to "break" into a legitimate travel page is to study it to see what is used and how it is handled. If your client has an interesting story or provides an unusual service, his publicity chances are good if you present the story honestly and creatively—even if he doesn't spend a dime on advertising.

Real Estate

Along with the population explosion and its attendant exodus to suburbia, the rash of new luxury apartment buildings, and expanded urban renewal programs, has also come the dynamic growth of commerical and industrial building. Although new housing starts have fallen off somewhat, a record number of homes have gone up over the last ten years. Hardly has the paint dried on a ten-story office building before it is torn down to make room for one thirty-stories high. New York, which hadn't seen a new hotel in forty years, suddenly was welcoming a half dozen within as many years. Other large cities are experiencing a similiar building boom.

Keeping the American public abreast of the fast-moving developments in this area has been the task of the real estate pages of the daily newspaper. On large newspapers, the real estate section rates equal billing with the busines and financial section, and the publicity man working in this area will receive preferred treatment, providing, of course, he has something to tell.

The real estate editor, like most other editors, is a specialist in his field. By choice or by chance, he has become thoroughly conversant with every aspect of the real estate business—from housing bills before Congress to who owned the corner lot where the blacksmith shop used to be. But first and foremost, he is a newspaperman, and although his field of interest is real estate, his primary concen is news.

He works with home builders, developers, real estate associations, architects, designers, mortgage brokers,— anyone and everyone engaged in any activity even remotely concerned with real estate. But what he wants from them is good solid news stories in their field—even a "scoop" or an "exclusive," once in a while to keep things lively. And he is always on the alert for good, interesting feature stories—a story that is not necessarily news, but offers interesting sidelights or background about people, places and things in the real estate news.

Here's where the publicity man comes in.

Glenn Fowler, Real Estate Editor of *The New York Times,* considers the publicity man a valuable assistant and rates the specialist in this field a notch or two higher than do other department editors. Mr. Fowler says it is essential that the publicity man know his client's business thoroughly before trying to service the real estate editor.

"I get the best story ideas from the publicity man who concentrates on this area," he says, "but I am shocked at the inadequacies of the others. Some of the largest public relations firms in town come to me with stories that show a remarkable lack of knowledge about their own clients' business, as well as of the needs of the real estate pages. Usually, their stories are inaccurate, unimaginative, and not thought through."

Always on the lookout for solid feature stories, Mr. Fowler observes:

"Many publicity men feed me the usual financial data and daily events which are important, but they seldom come up with a solid feature idea. Apparently they don't take the time to dig into the company as a good reporter will for the unusual or interesting. Yet, here is where a publicity man can perform his greatest service to his client—and to the editor.

"Let's face it. The company doesn't really need the publicity man to issue the usual once-a-year financial statements. They could do that themselves. What they do need is a publicity man who can come up with angles that make good features as well."

Mind Over Matters

In digging around for features, keep the newspaper's "policy" in mind. Some papers are "for" certain things like urban renewal, slum clearance, public housing, while others are "against." Keep these in mind when you angle a feature story toward the department. Don't overload your story. Every newspaper in the country has space problems these days.

Don't restrict your thinking to the Sunday sections or

pages put out by the real estate editor. He writes a lot of the stuff that appears in the news columns during the week, too. If your story is timely, get it to him while it's still fresh. And you need not limit your contacts to the real estate editor, but may feel free to communicate with any of his staff, too. (On small newspapers where the editor is his own, entire staff, he'll be glad to have you working as a stringer for him!)

At *The Times,* Mr. Fowler says, "I have no objections if the publicity man goes directly to the reporter first. In fact, I encourage it. I couldn't possibly listen to every idea or read every release that pours in every day. If the publicity man sparks an idea with a member of my staff, the idea will have had the benefit of his thinking and development by the time it comes to my attention.

"Often, a publicity man comes to us with a story that is too weak to stand alone, but we get a very usable feature by expanding it to cover the entire field, rather than a single company, and the publicity man's client still gets his break. This is one reason we encourage publicists to come in with ideas. I'm looking for a good page, not pride of authorship."

The Obituary

At one time or another, every publicity man will be called upon to place an obituary in the newspaper.

Although obituaries usually appear on one particular page each day, the actual copy is processed through the city desk and is written by a rewrite man. Sometimes a general assignment man will get on the phone to check out a few details.

A great proportion of the obituary reports come into

the newspaper by telephone, and this is one time when the "don't phone" rule does not apply, since time is important. However, if you can, it is best to send your story as a press release by messenger. One way to make certain that your story will get all the papers when you are up against deadlines is to give it to the Associated Press local man. If AP carries it, all the newspapers will get it.

The prominence or importance of the person who has died will determine how much space the editor will allow for the obit. Most of them run about an inch long. Others, of course, may make Page One.

This will be a matter for the editor to decide, and the publicity man should content himself with presenting his story simply and factually. An obituary release should contain the following information:

1. Name of the deceased
2. Age (This is one area where reporters sometimes have difficulty with publicity men or families— they do not always want to divulge the age)
3. Time, date, and place of death
4. Cause of death
5. Professional and personal background
6. Survivors
7. Funeral arrangements

(Some newspapers list funeral arrangements as a necessary part of the story; others feel that this information properly belongs in the "paid" death announcement columns. A Long Island (N.Y.) newspaper refuses to carry an obituary unless the family also buys a paid notice. Check the local obituary page to find out how this is handled.)

A typical obituary release should read something like this:

"John Brown, a partner in the construction firm of Brown and Yates and Company, 52 Wall Street, died yesterday of cerebral hemorrhage at City Hospital after a brief illness. He was 52 years old.

"Mr. Brown, a builder of residential homes, was honored last year by the Architectural Forum for his 'outstanding contribution to better living.' He also served for the past three years as secretary of the Homebuilders Association.

"Mr. Brown was a graduate of Columbia University and served as a lieutenant in the United States Army during World War II.

"Survivors include his widow, Lillian; a son, John Jr.; and a daughter, Mrs. Mary Ann Rodgers, all of Scarsdale, N. Y."

If the deceased is prominent in his community, include a photograph with the release.

Gardening

Into the office of the Garden Editor of the daily newspaper flows a steady stream of news from nurserymen, landscape architects, seed growers, nursery catalog people, power equipment manufacturers, garden clubs and associations. New products, new gadgets for gardening, new ideas are laid before the eyes of the editor, and chances are, on a large newspaper, much of this material will wind up in the circular file (the wastebasket) because the senders have not familiarized themselves with the policy of the paper to which they are sending the release.

On some large papers, the garden clubs will find their activities merely listed in a column. In small towns and on smaller papers, this kind of news may receive more space, but it will be found on the woman's page.

Some important dailies may list new garden products in a column but make a practice of not giving space to a new product unless it is so outstanding or so important that the public should be told about it. On such a newspaper, product publicity does not exist. There is a good reason for this—gardening is one area where gadgets grow like weeds, and the department could soon be overgrown with items or stories about such products.

A round-up story, such as one on new types of swimming pools, offers the publicity man an open door, for such a story would of necessity have to tell the reader not only what types of pools are available, but who makes them.

On smaller newspapers, where competition for space is not so keen, the publicist stands a better chance, especially if he uses a little imagination. Try to develop stories that illustrate the uses of you client's product without being flatly commerical. An article on the control crab grass, for instance, would be informative and useful to the reader. The fact that your client produces a super-special crabgrass killer can be slipped in inoffensively.

Publicity chairmen for the local garden clubs and conservation groups can command space if they report in detail. Much of what a speaker has to say at special meetings might interest many a reader who doesn't belong to the group. For instance, don't just sum up the speaker by saying:

"Mrs. Deborah Goldenrod spoke on roses."

Tell the editor what she said about the care of roses. When should they be pruned? Where should they be planted? How often should they be sprayed? Which varieties have the loveliest scent? Which the most intense colors?

The principles outlined in Chapters 5 and 6 on press releases and pictures apply here, as everywhere else.

Editorial Page

The editorial page is the mouthpiece of the newspaper editor, a public forum where he and his readers exchange views and discuss the issues of the day. On the editorial page appear not only the editorials which present the newspaper's point of view, but also letters from readers, columns of humor or light reading interest, columns of comment and sometimes essays and poetry. Cartoons help to make the point of the lead editorial vivid.

The editorial itself serves a number of purposes: To mold public opinion and keep opinion out of the news columns, to inform, explain, interpret, argue, urge action, crusade, persuade and, often, to entertain.

It is here that the newspaper's policy is enunciated, and newspaper policy is something with which every publicist and publicity chairman should be familiar, for in many instances, it has a direct bearing upon the paper's use or non-use of certain publicity material.

A thorough reading of the editorial page of several issues of the newspaper will tell you just how provincial the paper is. In some, the editorials deal primarily with events of national, international and universal importance. Local issues may rate a secondary position. In others, the emphasis is on issues of a purely local nature. Most newspapers espouse certain, generally-accepted ideas—they're for motherhood and against sin—but the range is wide when it comes to the kind and measure of their support on matters of public welfare and the common good.

Needless to say, a "break" in a newspaper editorial is probably the most prestigious publicity that can be given any client or organization. The importance and weight of the editorials are not used lightly, however, and rarely will a commercially-inspired idea break into print in the editorial column.

As Alden Hoag, chief editorial writer for *The Boston Herald* expressed it in *PR Reporter,* publicity people are "up against the world" in vying for editorials in daily newspapers. Publicity men for the non-profit organizations have had the greatest success in gaining this kind of support, and many editorial pages take cognizance of important community events. The Red Cross, the Mothers March on Polio, the launching of the Community Chest and United Fund drives have all earned editorial page support. However, other similarly worthy undertakings may also stand a chance.

According to Hoag, with the exception of a few large metropolitan papers, "most dailies across the country are starting to give more editorial treatment to local events."

The best way to get an editorial is to ask for it. Frank R. Rosenau, editorial writer for *The Springfield* (Mass.) *Union,* says publicity people should mark an extra copy of news releases that might warrant editorial treatment, and send it to the newspaper's editorial writer. Rosenau emphasized that the release should be accompanied by a cover letter giving reasons why it merits such attention.

Most editorial writers are anonymous—that is, they get no by-line and their names are seldom known to people outside the newspaper business. But they are skilled analysts as well as skilled writers, and experts in translating the complexities of today's living into terms that the average man will understand. The editorial writer knows how his readers think, live and act, and he views the passing parade with sympathy and understanding.

He is, therefore, no dreamer in an ivory tower. He is a man who knows the score. Don't bombard him with releases, don't try to softsoap him or tug at his sympathies, but don't be awed, either, into complete silence by the truly great influence he wields.

Study the newspaper's policy, then tell the editorial writer what it is you have to "sell." If he thinks it deserves editorial support, he will bring the matter up in the day's editorial conference, and your client or organization may have won a powerful ally.

Press Associations

Now that the world is shrinking a little every day, more and more newspapers are broadening their coverage horizons, opening their columns to news from all over the nation and the world. Today, even small newspapers probably contain as much news furnished by outside sources as is gathered by their own local staffs. Although medium-sized and large papers may have some staff in various parts of the country or the world, most of them depend primarily upon the wire services for their national and international news coverage.

There are a number of organizations listed as press associations and offering news services, but the three best known in this country are Associated Press, United Press International and The Reuter Agency. (Tass, the Soviet press association, is also familiar, but it is doubtful that any of our readers need to worry about working with that organization.)

To the professional publicist and the part-time publicity chairman, AP and UPI are the important associations.

Associated Press is the older and larger of the two, servicing more than 7,000 clients throughout the world. It is the largest cooperative news gathering and distributing agency in the world, developed from a loose federation of news agencies operating in various parts of the United States before 1892.

Owned by its members on a cooperative basis, it has no stock, makes no profits and declares no dividends. Each member pays his fair share of the operating expense.

United Press International is a private business enterprise formed in 1958 from the United Press, founded in 1907, and the International News Service, founded in 1909. E. W. Scripps, founder of United Press, first introduced the principle of selling reports to newspapers on a non-exclusive basis even when this resulted in servicing papers in competition with his own.

The techniques of working with the wire services are the same as for working with the newspaper directly, except for one important difference. To make the wire services, your story must have national or statewide interest or appeal. You must have the kind of story—or picture—that will catch the eye of the reader in North Loup, Nebr., as well as in San Francisco or New York.

In large cities, the wire services can be used to advantage when time is an important factor. If the story is carried on the AP and UPI wires, you know it will go into the newspaper offices all over town, and possibly get there more quickly than if you delivered the story yourself or sent it by special messenger.

Getting the story on the wire, of course, is no guarantee that it will be printed. That decision rests with the editor of the local paper. However, such is the prestige of the press association that the mere fact of seeing it "on the wire" can sway the editor in his decision.

11

NEWS IDEAS

As WE HAVE stressed in other chapters, before you can hope to see your "special interest" in print, you must have something newsworthy to say about it. The degree and importance of this news, however, is a matter of opinion —and there is often a wide gulf between the opinions of editors and publicity men. What you might rate as top priority news—nothing less than earth-shaking, in fact— might be considered marginal or worthless by an editor. This is the time when a publicity man must think like a reporter, selecting only the real "news" of his project and servicing it to the newspaper.

In previous chapters, we have touched upon some news-making events and have examined in detail the mechanics of servicing this news to the newspapers. This chapter will concern itself with news-making ideas that have not been touched upon up to now. Some of these may provide you with news starters for future stories.

Most special events generate a number of genuine news angles which can legitimately be exploited. It would be impossible to set down a formula to determine all the possibilities of a special event, since each involves a different set of circumstances, but we can set down a list of basic story ideas that, with some variations, will fit into the publicity pattern of almost any special event.

The following examples should give you a take-off point for your general publicity program, and can serve as a yardstick by which to measure the news possibilities of other activities in which your organization may engage.

1. The decision to stage the event

This story announces that such-and-such event is going to be held, names the projected date, and gives the time and place. It describes the exact nature of the event and stresses its objectives, its reason for being. It covers the steps leading to the decision to hold the event, and it gives a detailed description of the sponsoring organization.

2. Appointment of general chairman

If the event is civic or non-profit in nature, and if it involves volunteer workers, this release should announce the appointment of the general coordinating chairman and name the officer who is making the announcement. In this story, you should review the chairman's position in the business or professional world, his position in the community, and the responsibilities of his participation in the special event. Include a direct quote from the new chairman, one that indicates his enthusiasm for the assignment and stresses his dedication to the objectives of the sponsoring organization or group. Include an endorsement of the chairman by the sponsoring group, perhaps by an official who praises the chairman's talents, reputation, experience and ability to accomplish the objectives of the event.

3. **Appointment of major committeemen**

If the event is civic or non-profit, this release should announce the appointments of committee chairmen or members of major committees, giving the professional and civic background and exact responsibilities of each in the event. Include a statement from the coordinating chairman extolling the virtues of these committeemen and welcoming them aboard. Note: If there are more than three major committee members, the list should be broken up and the announcements should be released at intervals—the most important assignments being announced first.

4. **Historical report**

This is a background story. It should cover in detail the history of the event, possibly listing other similar events held in the past, their results, their impact on the growth and development of the community or of the company or sponsoring organization. Accompanying photographs might be unearthed from old files, depicting a person, scene or event of years past—100, 50, or 25 years ago. Such photos might illustrate "how times have changed," "then and now," or "then and tomorrow." They could cover the "old and new" of products, streets, buildings, hair styles, dress, modes of transportation.

5. **Biography of group sponsoring event**

Another background story, this discusses the sponsoring group, its history and progress, its position in the community, industry, or profession, and its role in the event. This story details the work of the group in products, service, philanthropy, or all three.

This story should also explain the philosophy and the goals underlying the group's activities—the particular event included. Photographs of the company or group officers, of the plant, store, home base, of products or laboratories, can accompany such a release.

6. Progress meeting

This story reports the first progress meeting, listing all the financial developments so far (does the group have to raise more money or is the special event over-subscribed already?) giving the highlights of any reports by individual chairmen. This story may stress either the negative or positive progress of the event, including, perhaps, an appeal for additional funds, workers, exhibits, historical data or other needed materials. A photograph could show committee members meeting in a well-known and popular restaurant, or a committee member displaying a check or some other item connected with the event such as a costume or flag, slogan, poster, etc.

7. New developments

Any development pertaining to the event has some news value. This might include: Names of new volunteers, retaining of consulting firms, announcements of personalities scheduled to participate or their arrival on scene, finishing touches being put to the plant, office, store, stadium, streets; posting of banners and displays, announcements of guest speakers and their topics. There could conceivably be several "new development" stories. How many appear in print will depend upon newspaper space available, time elapsing before the event, and other highly individual considerations.

Photographs could include head shots of speakers or entertainers. Action pictures might show dignitaries or city officials buying the first tickets, workmen nailing in the last board or laying the last brick, children tacking up a sign, chairman welcoming a celebrity at plane or train, mountains of merchandise piled on the street or at the delivery entrance, fixtures going in, training sessions, and so forth.

8. Recap of activities

Recapitulate all the significant details of the event, the what, where, when, who, how, and sometimes why. Announce any last-minute changes or final developments. This story is a guide as well as a reminder for your hoped-for audience.

Following is a list of events and the news possibilities that can come out of them. We list only the news hook. We expect you to follow all the journalistic rules governing the composition of a proper press release.

Luncheons

1. Date, time and place of event

2. Anticipated attendance and the nature of the event
3. Guest speakers and their discussion topics
4. Objectives of the luncheon: To pay tribute to a person, place or thing; to raise money; to launch a promotion period.
5. Special entertainment or entertainers
6. Honored guests: Their names and positions in business and community (mayor, police chief, corporation head, movie star, union leader, etc.)
7. Special menus: Imported foods, rare delicacies, original creations, etc.
8. Reception before the luncheon: List invited guests, where reception is to be held, time, and entertainment, if any

Conventions

1. Date, time and location of event
2. Anticipated attendance, geographic representation
3. Unusual meetings in connection with convention
4. Special forums, guest speakers, special films
5. Luncheons, dinners, banquets, or dances planned
6. List of outgoing officers, nominees
7. Formal opening ceremonies, welcoming speech by city or company official
8. New developments in ideas, products, equipment, personnel
9. Results of voting: New officers, adoption of rules, laws, and resolutions
10. Closing dinner, dance, speaker

Trade Shows

1. Date, time and location of the event

2. Anticipated attendance
3. List of exhibitors and nature of business
4. Unusual displays and exhibits
5. Special meetings: Kind, expected attendance, guest speakers, subjects discussed, when and where
6. Special showings: Live and filmed; when and where
7. New products, new developments in field, new techniques, inventions
8. New selling techniques, results of unusual sales
9. Famous and important visitors expected and attending
10. Formal opening ceremonies: When, where; dignitaries who will officiate, attend or speak

Store Openings

1. Date, time, location of the opening
2. Cost of construction, merchandise stocked, cost of land on which store is built; possibly historical background if land has one (the old sports field, original site of the grist mill, reclaimed marsh land, take off of historical flight or site of famous battle, etc.)
3. Anticipated opening day attendance
4. Special giveaways: Balloons, refreshments, flowers, toys, books, pen and pencil sets, etc.
5. Transportation and travel accessibility: List all bus, subway, train and automobile routes; description of parking facilities (capable of handling 1,000 cars, etc.)
6. Special transportation for opening day only: Chartered busses, horse and buggy ride, etc.

7. Management and personnel profiles, with accent on local people who will be involved in new store operation

8. Design features of new building; names of the architects, designers, style of design, modern features, worth of antiques, unusual additions or innovations

9. Entertainment and special programs for opening day or week; names of entertainers; time and places

10. Unique services: Restaurant, milk bar, beauty parlor, baby tenders, dog sitters, roof garden, self service

11. Unusual opportunities for those attending event: sale slashed prices, special discounts, etc.

12. Unique merchandise: Styles, brands, other facts

13. Opening day ceremonies planned: Time, location, duration, etc.

14. Entertainers scheduled to appear: Names, background, nature of performance: will they stay around to autograph, special guests of some local socialite or city official?

15. Participation in opening day ceremonies: Local band members and director, town or city officials and other dignitaries, women's clubs, civic club representative, school groups, clergy

Other Openings

1. Date, time, location of opening

2. Organizations participating

3. Historical data: Other openings or similar events, history of the location, meaning of the date selected, historical significance to the community

4. Unique employee facilities

5. Plant tours or open house: Full details

6. Entertainment features planned: Parade, carnival, fireworks, competitions, community singing, pageants or tableaux

7. The parade: Its components; parade route, starting time, estimated number of bands and marchers, floats, theme

8. Fireworks: Cost of display, length of show, unique features, location of firing; location of viewing

9. Participation: Merchant, civic, religious groups, military, nature of their participation, same for individuals if size of contribution warrants

10. Architectural and physical details

For the business firm or company here is a list of news-making ideas which appeared in an issue of *Business Management* magazine, a publication dedicated to the "how" of business affairs.

1. **History of company**

   Anniversaries of company, senior officers, or long-term employees
   New building or radical change in office layout
   Accomplishments in sales or products
   Banquets or awards dinners

2. **Manufacturing**

   New products, methods or processes
   New raw materials—origins and uses
   Research findings for product or method improvement

Service improvement
Patents acquired
New safety devices
Time or labor-saving developments

3. Organization

Company policies that may be affected by city, state or government policy changes
Community problems solved
Dealer relations
Outstripping competitors
New stock issues
Company clubs or organizations
Policies on credit, deliveries, return of goods or exchanges
Distribution, merchandising or advertising methods
Sales promotion programs
Research that proves quality of product
Employee training programs

4. Personalities

Statements from company officers on new developments or policy
Important talks or speeches by company personnel
Individual accomplishments of personnel
Visits by famous people
Visits by groups or associations
Promotions
Employees who perform interesting services outside the company

5. Research

Reports of discoveries
New equipment or facility development
Progress, industry and past research reports
Trends in sales, production, employment
Projected plans and programs
Joint educational, industrial or government programs
Thesis presentation and newly published information

6. Products and service

New uses for existing products
Lower price due to efficient operation or lower-cost materials
Unusual product uses
Bids or awards
Prizes for products
New designs, trademark or package
Large new contracts for services
Comparison analyses for ruggedness, economy, etc.

7. Promotion, distribution

Sales conventions or trade shows
New product introduction
New distributors or dealers
New areas of distribution
Unit and dollar volume of sales
Dealer exhibits, surveys, fairs, showings
Sales success stories
Contests, new offers, new premiums

8. Trademarks, slogans, symbols

New trademark or redesigned old one
New slogan
Endorsement of products or services by prominent
figures
New company symbol

9. Activity of employees

Interesting backgrounds, hobbies, or accomplish-
ments of employees below the executive level
Increase in number of employee benefits
New recreational facilities or activities
Employee awards
Safety or security records
Retirements, births, deaths
Civic activities

10. Community activity

Local news which relates to company
Community exhibits in which company has taken
part
Local election to office of company official

12

GLOSSARY OF

NEWSPAPER AND PUBLICITY TERMS

AD	Paid advertisement.
ADD	Additional news material to be appended to a story.
ADVANCE	A story concerning a future event.
AGATE	Type which measures 5½ points in size. Fourteen agate lines equal one column inch, and newspaper columns and advertising are measured by agate lines.
AGATE LINE	See above.
AM's	Morning newspapers.
ANGLE	A specific point of view applied to a story or idea.
AP	Associated Press.
ART	Newspaper illustrations (photographs, drawings, charts, maps, etc.).
ASSIGNMENT	A reporter's designated task.
BEAT	A reporter's regularly assigned territory for news cover-

	age—police, courts, labor, etc. Also a "scoop," a story printed only by one newspaper.
BLOW-UP	An enlargement.
BOIL DOWN	To reduce copy to fit space limitations in the newspaper.
BREAK	Used in publicity to mean getting a story or photograph printed in a newspaper. A story "breaks" when it is available for publication.
BY-LINE	Name of writer or reporter appearing directly above his story.
CANNED COPY	Syndicated material or material received from publicity offices or press agents.
CAPS	Contraction for "capital letters." The small letters are "lower case."
CAPTION	Descriptive information given under photographs, illustrations or diagrams.
CENTER SPREAD	An editorial or advertising layout occupying the center pages of a newspaper.
CLEAN COPY	Copy needing little or no revision.
CLIPS	Clippings from the newspapers or the morgue files.
COLUMN	A department regularly pub-

COPY

COPY NEGATIVE

COVER

CREDIT LINE

CUT

CUTLINE

DAY SIDE

lished. Also a vertical row of type.

Any text—advertising, editorial, photographic or illustration—that is to be printed.

A photographic copy of an existing photograph, used when making prints in quantity. Necessary when only a print, not a negative, is available.

What a reporter or photographer does when appearing in person to gather information or pictures for a story.

A line of type accompanying a picture or story, giving its source.

To cut is to shorten a story. The word also designates a newspaper engraving mounted on a block, used for reproducing drawings or photographs.

Used by some newspapers to designate the caption material under a cut.

Reporters, photographers and other newspaper personnel who work during the daytime.

DEAD	News material or type that is no longer usable.
DEADLINE	The time when all copy must be in the hands of the newspaper if it is to appear in the next edition. Also the time when an edition goes to press.
DIRTY COPY	Stories containing many errors, badly written or heavily edited.
DOUBLE TRUCK	An editorial or advertising layout made up as one unit, covering two facing pages which are not in the center of the paper.
EDITION	Newspapers printed during a single press run. Some papers print as many as seven editions.
EXCLUSIVE	A story published by one newspaper only.
FEATURE	Stories stressing the human side of the news, but not necessarily spot news,
FILLER	Unimportant material that can be used any time to fill up space.
FIRST DAY STORY	A current story; one that is being published for the first time.
FLACK	Slang for press agent.

FOLLOW-UP	A story giving developments on one printed earlier.
FUTURE	Memorandum of a future event.
GLOSSY	Photographic print with a shiny surface, necessary for newspaper reproduction.
GHOST	One who writes stories or speeches accredited to someone else.
GRAPEVINE	Source of rumors. Also copy which has been set and can be used at any time as filler.
HALF TONE	A picture that is photographed on metal through a screen and then etched, a process giving it shades or tones like a photograph.
HANDOUT	A statement prepared for publication. Publicity material handed out by publicist to reporters or photographers during a special event.
HEAD	Short for headline.
HEADLINE	Heading of a news story.
HEAD SHOT	Photograph of a person from the shoulders up. Also called a "mug shot."
HOLD FOR RELEASE	Instruction which is placed on copy to be set but not printed until the editor in charge or the PR man sending out the release says so.

214

HOT NEWS	Up-to-the-minute and important news.
HUMAN INTEREST	A news story or feature involving people and appealing to the readers' emotions.
INSERT	An additional sheet or sheets of copy to be inserted in a story already sent to the composing room.
INTERVIEW	A conference with an individual or several persons for the purpose of obtaining news.
JUNKET	Trip for reporters, sponsored and paid for by some special-interest group.
KILL	To cut out of copy; to destroy a story already in type.
LAYOUT	A sheet ruled into columns, representing a page of the newspaper and indicating where stories, advertisements and art are to be placed.
LEAD	The introduction—first sentence or first paragraph— of a story. A lead might also be a tip on a story.
LEG MAN	A reporter who gathers the news but does not necessarily write it.
LIBRARY	The files of newspaper clippings and other reference materials.

215

LINE CUT	An engraving of a line drawing or a line of lettering made by photographing it, but not photographing it through a screen as in a half tone.
MAKEUP	The placement of stories, pictures and advertisements in a newspaper page.
MAT	Short for matrix which is the papier-mache mold of a page of type, or of a single story, in one-column, two-column, etc., width. The material is reproduced from the mat by casting it in type metal.
MORGUE	A reference or file of newspaper clippings and other useful reference material.
MUST	A word every publicity man dreams of seeing on his copy; the editor's instructions that it must be printed without fail.
NIGHT SIDE	That portion of the newspaper staff that works at night.
OBIT	Obituary
OFF THE RECORD	Information given but not to be published.
OVERNIGHT	An assignment made for the following day.
OVERSET	Where a lot of publicity material winds up: type that

	has been set and is left over after the paper has been filled.
P.A.	Press agent.
PAD	To stretch out a story by adding unnecessary details.
PAYOLA	Special gratituities given to individuals for performing their jobs.
PIX	Pictures.
PLUG	A publicity term meaning a mention in a newspaper or on a radio or television broadcast. It is most commonly associated with publicity mentions in columns.
PM's	Afternoon newspapers.
POLICY	A newspaper's stand on any issue, or company's or organization's position on a given subject.
PR	Public relations.
PUFF	Used by newspapermen to describe out-and-out publicity copy which appears in print or which is submitted to an editor.
QUERY	A correspondent's (or free lance or publicity person's) written or telegraphed synopsis of a story that exists and indicating something of the nature of the story. An

editor will then tell the correspondent how many words to send, or accept or reject the outsider's idea.

RELEASE
A publicity story which is sent to a newspaper.

REPRINT
A copy of a printed story. Also any material which has appeared for the first time in the late editions of the paper, and is therefore not usable in the early editions of the next day's paper.

RETOUCHING
A process of touching up a photograph to correct imperfections, eliminate unnecessary or confusing details, etc.

REWRITE
To write a story that is telephoned into the newspaper by a leg man; also to write a story again to improve it, lengthen or shorten it, or bring it up to date.

ROP
Run of the paper. A picture that stands on its own, without an accompanying story, and can run anywhere in the paper.

SCOOP
An exclusive story printed only by one paper—one that other newspapers would like to have got their hands on, too.

SCRIPT	Written dialogue used in radio, television programs or by speakers at special events.
SHORTS	One or two-paragraph stories; relatively unimportant brief stories.
SIDEBAR	Stories touching upon the fringe areas of interest in connection with a major story.
SLANT	The emphasis which is placed upon a particular aspect of a policy or other story.
SPACE	A commodity that is bought by the advertiser, sold by the publisher for display and advertising, and hoped-for by the publicity man for the story he has sent in.
SPLIT PAGE	First page of the second section of the newspaper.
SPOT NEWS	Unexpected, important, live news.
SPREAD	A major story and its auxiliary stories; a layout of pictures connected with one story.
SQUIB	A brief news item.
STET	Copy editor and proof readers term meaning "let it stand" and used to indicate to the compositor that an ed-

iting change that has been marked and now cannot be erased, should be disregarded, and the copy should be set as it was written.

STORY

An article written by a reporter.

STRAIGHT NEWS

An account of news facts, without embellishments or feature interest.

STRINGER

A reporter or correspondent working for the newspaper on a free-lance basis. He may cover stories on assignment or he may cover them on his own, but he is usually paid on the basis of the story. These stories used to be clipped and pasted together to make a long string, and the correspondent was paid so much an inch.

STYLE BOOK

Rules of writing, editing, spelling and punctuation which make up the "style" of the newspaper.

SYNDICATE

An association which, either in conjunction with a newspaper, or as an independent organization, buys or sells news stories, features and other material for newspapers.

220

TABLOID — A small-sized newspaper. usually half the size of a full seven-column newspaper. The limited space gave rise to a particular style of news presentation which is also called by the same term.

TEAR SHEET — Pages containing an article or advertisement, torn from the newspaper or magazine after publication.

THIRTY — The end of the story or series.

TIE-IN — The cooperative efforts of two or more groups in one promotion; also material previously printed but incorporated in current story to refresh the readers' memories.

TIGHT PAPER — Publicity man's nightmare. A paper so filled with ads that a reduction of news space is necessary and therefore the total elimination of anything not strictly news.

TIME COPY — Copy that is set and then held for later use.

TIP — Information suggesting a news story.

TYPO — Typographical error; an error occurring when printers are setting type.

UPI — United Press International.

WHEN ROOM	Term meaning the story may be used at any time.
WHIFF	Like puff, publicity material of small news value.
WIDE-OPEN PAPER	The opposite of a tight paper.

13

PRESS CLIPPINGS

THE PUBLICIST OR the publicity chairman who wants to know—or show—how wide a press coverage he obtained for his client or organization needs the services of a press clipping bureau. This is true whether his motivations are to keep the record straight, to satisfy his ego, or just to fill an empty scrapbook. For without tangible, visual evidence in the form of the printed word, the full effects of a highly successful publicity program often can be dissipated.

Remember the old brain twizzler: If a great force moved a huge boulder in the heart of the Sahara Desert, but no human being was on hand to observe this wonder, did the boulder actually move? It is the function of a press clipping service to watch boulders move.

Readers for a clipping service go over hundreds of newspapers and magazines daily in search of mentions of specific persons, organizations, products, or causes. When the item is found, it is clipped, affixed to a paper tab carrying the name of the publication and the date on which it appeared, and forwarded to the publicist or client.

Although press clipping services do not come cheaply, they are generally within the reach of most groups and can be retained by the year, the month, or for just one particular job. If you are a publicist in a large city where there are several newspapers putting out several editions, or if you service newspapers on a regional or national basis, a clipping bureau is almost a must. No single publicity man—not even a fully-staffed publicity organization—can possibly read every edition of every newspaper every day.

Don't—as some publicity men do—try to solve this problem by asking editors to mail you a copy of the story if they run it. Most editors not only will not honor the request—for lack of time, if nothing else—but they will frankly resent it.

The implication of such a request is that, although you want the editor to run your publicity, you just can't find the time to read his newspaper. Such a request also suggests that you have sent out a "broadside" mailing, and this tends to lessen its charm for the editor.

Techniques of working with a clipping service are fairly simple:

1. Provide the service with a list of key names to look for: company name, product name, brand name, personality, organization, etc.
2. Provide a list of the kind of publications you are servicing.
3. Inform the service of the general geographic area to which you are directing your publicity efforts.
4. Give them the subject or subjects you are promoting.
5. Keep them informed of the timing of your publicity mailings.
6. Provide them with a few copies of each release.

In an article in *P R Quarterly,* Harold L. Gerberg, General Manager of Burrelle's Press Clipping Bureau, the oldest and largest such service in the world, offers this checklist for the publicity man who wants to help the clipping bureau produce a greater percentage of pick-ups.

1. Keep in close touch with the bureau unless your account is one that appears frequently in the press.

2. Be sure the bureau is on your mailing list.

3. Advise the bureau when your publicity releases are going to selected media.

4. Notify the bureau whenever you mail out a release which you want handled differently from the routine instructions placed with the bureau.

5. Send a memorandum or make a call to the bureau when your release contains the mention of a new product or new brand name. This is essential because sometimes a newspaper may print the new product name without mentioning the name of the manufacturer, and there would be no way for the bureau reader to know this. It would be a good idea to add the "keyword" or the new brand name to the reader's instructions to make certain the story will be recognized.

6. A copy of a syndicated column, by-lined article, or mat story should be in the hands of the bureau a few days before you expect it to appear in print. If you can't do this, telephone or send a note or wire.

7. It is no longer true that bureaus are two weeks behind in their reading. A bureau must be notified of the release no later than the day you expect it to appear, since some papers are read the same day or the day following publication, and many are read within four or five days.

8. Your orders to the clipping bureau should contain as few restrictions or conditions as possible.

Be as specific as you can. If your instructions are ambiguous, the reader will have to use his or her own judgment, and it may not always correspond with what you had in mind.

9. Examine the first few shipments of clippings immediately to determine whether the bureau understands exactly what you want.

John P. French, partner in the Luce Press Clipping Bureau of Topeka, Kansas, amplifies this last point in *Public Relations Journal*:

"Use your complaints intelligently," he says. "Return any clippings contrary to what was requested. These are analyzed at once. If any change in an order is required, it can be made quickly.

"Sometimes people hire a bureau, let it work for three months or more, and then write to stop the order because the service 'has been terrible from the beginning.' Nobody gains this way."

There are a number of good press clipping services from which to choose. Here are the major bureaus in the field: Burrelle's Press Clipping Bureau, New York City; American Trade Press, New York City; Bacon's Clipping Bureau, Chicago, Ill.; Luce Press Clipping Bureau, Topeka, Kan.; Press Intelligence, Washington, D.C.; and Romeike Press Clipping Bureau, New York City.

Even though you do employ the services of one of these, or other bureaus, chances are you still will never see 100 per cent coverage of your publicity labors. Although these organizations are remarkably accurate, you will be inclined to feel that your story probably received wider coverage than the clippings would indicate. To some degree, you would be right.

For the clipping service, like any other service, is performed by human beings, and the human margin for error must always be taken into consideration. People do the reading, and people can make mistakes. There are, however, other factors contributing to the loss of clippings.

Burrelle's Harold Gerberg lists some of the reasons clippings are "lost:"

1. There is the distinct possibility that even if the material was printed by various media, the key word or key phrase may have been deleted by the editors. This would make certain releases extremely difficult to recognize.

2. Frequently, an item is used in only one edition of a particular newspaper, and currently it is not practical for a clipping service to subscribe to every edition of every newspaper in the country. Most bureaus, however, do subscribe to several editions of all major papers.

3. The item may have appeared prior to the time the order was placed or prior to the time the bureau was advised that it should appear.

4. Occasionally, an item is printed two or three months after the bureau has been advised to be on the alert for it. Unless it is a constantly active subject in the press, the readers cannot be expected to recognize a photo or release that was shown to them months before it actually appeared in print.

5. While magazine and newspaper subscription lists are carefully maintained and checked, a certain percentage are lost in the mails despite all precautions.

6. (a) In the case of syndicated columns, a paragraph appearing in a New York City paper or in

the paper in which it originated is frequently omitted in the out-of-town journals.

(b)   Syndicated columns, mat stories and feature items are often purchased in a "package deal" but are used at the discretion of the editor. Consequently, the entire column or story containing mention of the subject requested may never appear.

INDEX

229

INDEX

INDEX